The Office Application Handbook

Laura Monsen

The Office Application Handbook

Copyright© 1998 by Que® Corporation.

All rights reserved. Printed in the United States of America. No part of this book may be used or reproduced in any form or by any means, or stored in a database or retrieval system, without prior written permission of the publisher except in the case of brief quotations embodied in critical articles and reviews. Making copies of any part of this book for any purpose other than your own personal use is a violation of United States copyright laws. For information, address Que Corporation, 201 W. 103rd Street, Indianapolis, IN, 46290. You may reach Que's direct sales line by calling 1-800-428-5331.

Library of Congress Catalog No.: 98-86991

ISBN: 0-7897-1829-4

This book is sold as is, without warranty of any kind, either express or implied, respecting the contents of this book, including but not limited to implied warranties for the book's quality, performance, merchantability, or fitness for any particular purpose. Neither Que Corporation nor its dealers or distributors shall be liable to the purchaser or any other person or entity with respect to any liability, loss, or damage caused or alleged to have been caused directly or indirectly by this book.

99 98   7 6 5 4 3 2

Interpretation of the printing code: the rightmost double-digit number is the year of the book's printing; the rightmost single-digit number, the number of the book's printing. For example, a printing code of 98-1 shows that the first printing of the book occurred in 1998.

All terms mentioned in this book that are known to be trademarks or service marks have been appropriately capitalized. Que cannot attest to the accuracy of this information. Use of a term in this book should not be regarded as affecting the validity of any trademark or service mark.

Screen reproductions in this book were created using Collage Plus from Inner Media, Inc., Hollis, NH.

Contents at a Glance

1 **New and Enhanced Microsoft Office Features Common to All Programs** 1

2 **Upgrading to Microsoft Word 95 and Word 97** 19

3 **Upgrading to Microsoft Excel 95 and Excel 97** 57

Table of Contents

1 New and Enhanced Microsoft Office Features Common to All Programs   1

Managing Files   2
    New Options When Opening Files   2
    Improved Methods for Locating Files   4
    New Options in the Save As Dialog Box   6
Editing and Drawing Enhancements   8
    AutoCorrect Feature Is Now Available in All Office Programs   8
    Using Office Art (Office 97 Only)   10
Expanded Online Help   12
    Revised Table of Contents and Index Help Screens   12
    Introducing the Answer Wizard and Office Assistant   14
    Online Help via the Internet (Office 97 Only)   16

2 Upgrading to Microsoft Word 95 and Word 97   19

What's New   20
    Word 95   20
    Word 97   20
Managing Files   22
    Exchanging Files Between Different Versions of Word   22
    Creating New Files Using the Built-in Templates   24
    Saving Files in HTML Format (Word 97 Only)   26
Editing Text   28
    Improved Spell Check and Grammar Options   28
Tables   30
    Table and Border Toolbars   30
    Drawing a Table (Word 97 Only)   32
    Distributing Rows and Columns Evenly in a Table (Word 97 Only)   34
    Changing Text Orientation in a Table (Word 97 Only)   36
Templates and Forms   38
    Using the Built-in Templates   38
    Creating Custom Templates   40
Font Enhancements   42
    New Font Effects (Word 97 Only)   42
    Applying Font Animation (Word 97 Only)   44
Tracking Revisions   46

Contents

Expanded Revision Marks (Word 97 Only) 46
Adding Comments (Word 97 Only) 48
Merging Documents (Word 97 Only) 50
Reviewing Document Changes 52
Saving Document Versions (Word 97 Only) 54

3 Upgrading to Microsoft Excel 95 and Excel 97 57

What's New 58
- Excel 95 58
- Excel 97 58

Managing Files 60
- Exchanging Files Created in Different Versions of Excel 60
- Creating New Files Using the Built-in Templates 62
- Saving Files in HTML Format (Excel 97 Only) 64

Editing and Formatting 66
- Merging Cells (Excel 97 Only) 66
- Indenting and Rotating Data (Excel 97 Only) 68
- AutoComplete 70
- Validating Data Entry (Excel 97 Only) 72
- Applying Conditional Formats (Excel 97 Only) 74
- Displaying and Reviewing Embedded Comments 76

Formulas and Functions 78
- Creating and Editing Formulas (Excel 97 Only) 78
- New Functions (Excel Only) 80

Analyzing Worksheets 82
- Filtering Lists 82
- Pivot Table Improvements 84

Templates 86
- Using the Built-in Templates 86
- Template Wizard with Data Tracking 88

Charts and Maps 90
- Creating Maps 90
- Improved Chart Wizard (Excel 97 Only) 92

Workgroup Features 94
- Sharing Workbooks 94
- Merging Workbooks (Excel 97 Only) 98

Importing and Exporting Data 100
- Converting Excel Data into Access 100
- Enhanced MS Query (Excel 97 Only) 102

Index 188

Publisher

Credits

John Pierce

Executive Editor
Jim Minatel

Director of Editorial Services
Carla Hall

Managing Editor
Thomas F. Hayes

Acquisitions Editor
Jill Byus

Development Editor
Rick Kughen

Production Editor
Heather E. Butler

Editors

Anne Owen, Tom Stevens

Technical Editor
Russ Jacobs

Book Designer
Ruth Harvey

Cover Designer
Dan Armstrong

Production Team
Nicole Ritch, Lisa Stumpf, Scott Tullis

Indexer
Cheryl A. Jackson

Book Concept
Tom Ebeling

Composed in Stone Serif and Helvetica by Que Corporation.

About the Author

Laura Monsen is a professional instructor with more than seven years experience teaching computer application classes. For the past five years she has been teaching a variety of spreadsheet, project management, database, and graphic application classes for Productivity Point International (PPI), a leader in computer software training solutions. She teaches at the PPI site in San Antonio, Texas.

Laura is the author of *Using Microsoft Excel 97* recently published by Que. She has been a contributing author on several other Que computer reference books including *Special Edition Using Microsoft Project 98*, *Special Edition Using Microsoft PowerPoint 97*, and *Special Edition Using Microsoft Project 95*. Additionally, she frequently consults and tutors on Excel, Project, and PowerPoint. Laura has a B.A. in Economics from the University of the South, Sewanee, Tennessee.

ECCE QUAM BONUM

Acknowledgments

Jill Byus led the team of Que professionals who defined and edited this book. Her assistance and flexibility in its production allowed me to concentrate solely on writing. Jill was responsible for coordinating all the rest.

Another important person instrumental in developing this book who deserves my thanks is Rick Kughen. His superb editing suggestions ensured the text remained focused and concise. Go Packers!

Dedication

This book is dedicated to one of the most genuine people I've known, Rose Mayfield. Her infectious sense of humor and zest for life lives on, even though she is no longer with us.

We'd Like to Hear from You!

Que Corporation has a long-standing reputation for high-quality books and products. To ensure your continued satisfaction, we also understand the importance of customer service and support.

Tech Support

If you need assistance with the information in this book or with a CD/disk accompanying the book, please contact Macmillan Technical Support by phone at 317-581-3833 or via email at `quecorp.com`.

Orders, Catalogs, and Customer Service

To order other Que or Macmillan Computer Publishing books, catalogs, or products, please contact our Customer Service Department at 800/428-5331 or fax us at 800/882-8583 (International Fax: 317/228-4400). Or visit our online bookstore at `http://www.mcp.com/`.

Introduction

THIS BOOK IS DESIGNED AS A QUICK REFERENCE for people migrating to one of the newer versions of Microsoft Office—Microsoft Office 95 or Microsoft Office 97. Whether you are moving from Microsoft Office 4.3 (for Windows 3.1) or Microsoft Office 95, this book will help you get started.

You can purchase several different editions of Microsoft Office, including Professional Edition, Standard Edition, and Small Business Edition (Office 97 only). Each edition comes with a specific set of applications. This book focuses on the four most common applications—Word, Excel, Access, and PowerPoint.

Each application in Microsoft Office has its own version number. The table below lists the applications and their version numbers.

Application	Microsoft Office 4.3	Microsoft Office 95	Microsoft Office 97
Word	Word 6.0	Word 7.0	Word 8.0
Excel	Excel 5.0	Excel 7.0	Excel 8.0
Access	Access 2.0	Access 7.0	Access 8.0
PowerPoint	PowerPoint 4.0	PowerPoint 7.0	PowerPoint 8.0

Although the applications have version numbers, they are most often referred to by the Microsoft Office version they are part of rather than the application version. For example, Word 95 is used instead of Word 7.0. When referring to applications, this book will use the Microsoft Office version to avoid any possible confusion.

Who Should Use This Book?

This book is for the person who is currently using Microsoft Office and needs a guide to locate the commands and features that have been relocated or enhanced. The focus is on the differences between the Microsoft Office versions. As a quick reference guide, this book will outline where to find a command or feature. For detailed explanations and step-by-step instructions on using the Microsoft Office applications, there are several excellent series of books published by Que:

- Using Series. Designed for the intermediate to advanced user, these books describe the most frequently used features in an application. *Using Microsoft Excel 97* is one of many books in this series.

- Special Edition Using Series. Designed for beginning to advanced user, these books describe each and every feature in an application. *Special Edition Using Microsoft Access 97* is one of many books in this series.

How This Book Is Organized

This book is divided into five sections. Within each section you will learn about new features in the application, how to convert files from previous versions of the application, and differences between each version. The sections are as follows:

- New and Enhanced Features, Common to All Programs. The emphasis in this section is on similar features available in all Microsoft Office applications. Learn about changes to the way you manipulate files, improved editing and drawing options, and the expanded online help in Microsoft Office.
- Upgrading to Word 95 and Word 97. The most important new features in Word are described in this section. Additionally, enhanced methods for creating and editing tables and templates, along with tracking document revisions is discussed.
- Upgrading to Excel 95 and Excel 97. This section describes the new editing and formatting options in Excel, the improved chart wizard, methods for sharing workbooks, and alternatives for importing and exporting data.

Conventions Used in This Book

Certain text formats and other conventions are used in *Migrating to Office 95 and Office 97* to help you use this book more easily. The following typefaces are used to distinguish specific text:

Typeface Conventions

Type Appearance	Meaning
bold	Examples of information that is typed. Also used to emphasize text.
italics	New terms or phrases when they are first defined. May also be used to emphasize text.
underlined characters	Indicates keyboard shortcuts for menu and dialog box commands.

Generally keys appear in this book just as they appear on the keyboard, such as Enter or Tab.

TIP Additional, helpful information that makes a procedure easier to perform or a feature easier to use is displayed in this format.

NOTE Additional, useful information is displayed in this format.

Throughout the topics covered in this book, you will see bold numbers, like this **1** followed by a button name, field name, or description that corresponds with a figure that follows. Simply match the bold number in the text with the same bold number on a figure.

New and Enhanced Microsoft Office Features Common to All Programs

Microsoft Office 95 and Office 97 possess many commands and features that are accessed and executed in the same way, regardless of the Office product you are using. This chapter introduces these new and enhanced features:

- **Managing Files.** Control the features of the Open dialog box, locate files quickly, and create new folders (directories) while saving files.

- **Editing and Drawing Enhancements.** AutoCorrect feature included in all programs.

- **Expanded Online Help.** Improved Table of Contents and Search Index interface, interactive help from the Answer Wizard and Office Assistant, and getting help from the Internet.

Managing Files
New Options When Opening Files

When you open files in Office 95 and Office 97, you will notice quite a change in the appearance of the Open dialog box. With one minor exception, the Office 95 and Office 97 dialog boxes are identical. The only difference is the Office 97 dialog box includes an icon to access the World Wide Web. The figures to the right show the Open dialog boxes for Office 4.3 (Figure 1.1) and Office 97 (Figure 1.2).

By default in Office 95 and Office 97, the files you create are stored in the My Documents folder. This enables you to quickly locate your files without having to remember which application you used to create the file. In Figure 1.1, several folders have been created and stored in separate files and by distinct categories.

Included in the Open dialog box in Figure 1.2 are a series of icons for locating files. You can **1** display the next level up in your list of folders (directories), **2** search the World Wide Web (available only in Office 97), **3** display a list of folders and files you frequently access (your "favorites"), and **4** add a folder or file to your list of "favorite" files.

Additionally, icons are available for changing the information you see regarding each folder or file. Your folders and files can be **5** displayed as a simple list of files, as **6** a list with detailed information about the files such as the name, size, type, and date the folder or file was last modified. You can also **7** display the Properties of a selected file, which includes information like Author, Date Created, Number of Pages, and Number of Revisions. With Word or PowerPoint files, you can **8** Preview the upper-left portion of the file in the preview window.

> **NOTE** In Excel, you must activate this property for each file you want to be able to preview; otherwise, a message appears in the preview window indicating "Preview Not Available." This feature is not available for Access databases.

The **9** Commands and Settings icon enables you to open a read-only copy of a file, sort your list of folders or files, and modify the properties of a file.

Another new feature of the Open dialog box is your ability to delete files directly from the Open dialog box. Deleted files are moved to the Recycle Bin in Office 95 and Office 97.

Converting files created in older versions of Microsoft Office will be addressed in the chapters devoted to each application (Word, Excel, Access, and PowerPoint).

New and Enhanced Microsoft Office Features Common to All Programs

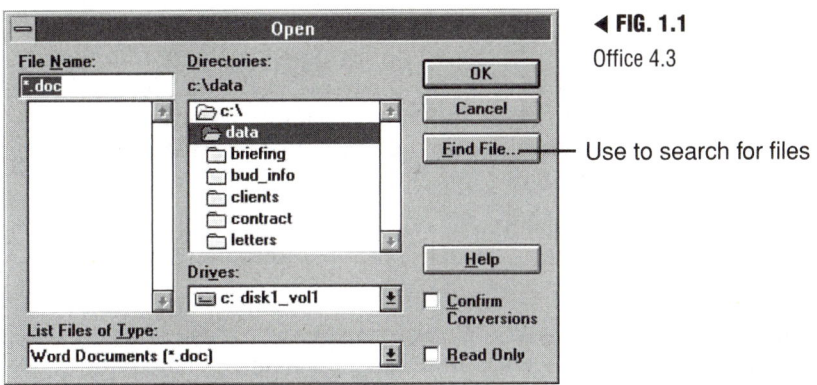

◀ **FIG. 1.1**
Office 4.3

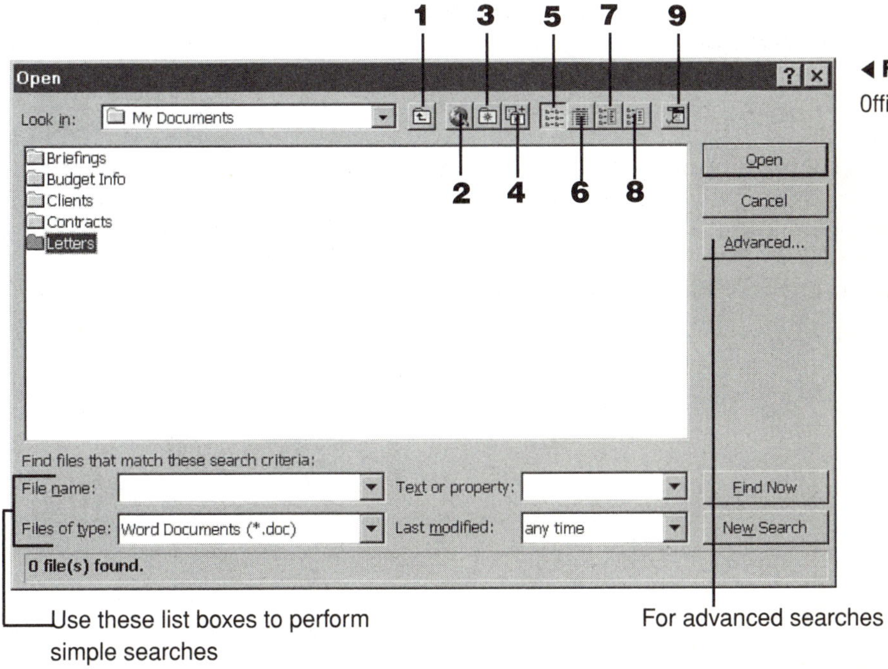

Use to search for files

◀ **FIG. 1.2**
Office 95/97

Use these list boxes to perform simple searches

For advanced searches

Managing Files

Improved Methods for Locating Files

Finding files is typically done through the Open dialog box. In all versions of Microsoft Office, you can search for files based on file type, summary information (a.k.a. Properties), and the timeframe a file was created or last modified. In Office 95 and Office 97, the Open dialog box includes the capability to perform simple searches based on these options. You can also perform advanced searches by using the Advanced button in the Open dialog box.

Figure 1.3 shows the Advanced Search dialog box for Office 4.3. This dialog box consists of **1** three tabs used to define a search: Location, Summary, and Timestamp.

Figure 1.4 shows the Advanced Find dialog box for Office 97, which is accessed from the Open dialog box. The Office 95 and Office 97 Advanced Find dialog boxes are identical. The Office 95 and Office 97 Advanced Find dialog box has consolidated the search capabilities from three tabs of the Office 4.3 Advanced Search dialog box. Additionally, the Advanced Find dialog box now includes the capability to define multiple criteria in the search, and to use **2** more detailed properties in the search. Office 95 and Office 97 applications keep track of a number of unique properties for each file.

> **TIP** **3** Include all subfolders for a more comprehensive search.

Figure 1.5 shows the Find All Files dialog box. In Windows 95, you can locate and open a file by using the Find feature. While there are several different ways to access the Find feature, one of the easiest is to click on the Start button and choose Find from the menu. You can then perform a **4** simple search using the three options tabs of the Find dialog box: Name & Location, Date Modified, and Advanced.

New and Enhanced Microsoft Office Features Common to All Programs

FIG. 1.3 ▶
Office 4.3—Advanced Search

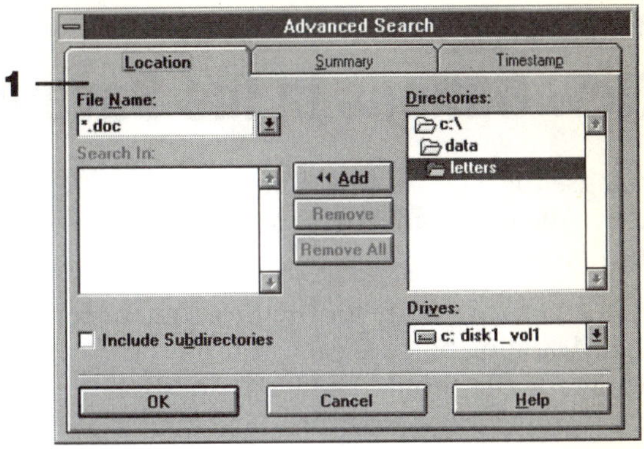

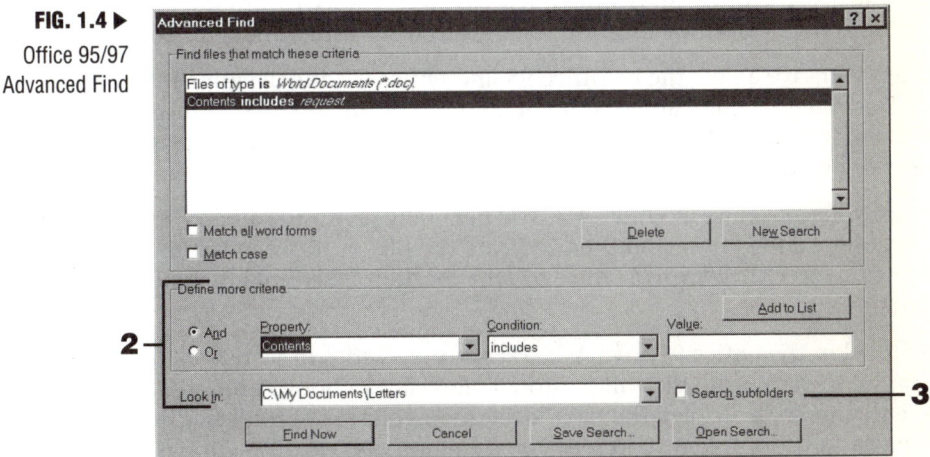

FIG. 1.4 ▶
Office 95/97 Advanced Find

FIG. 1.5 ▶
Find All Files dialog box

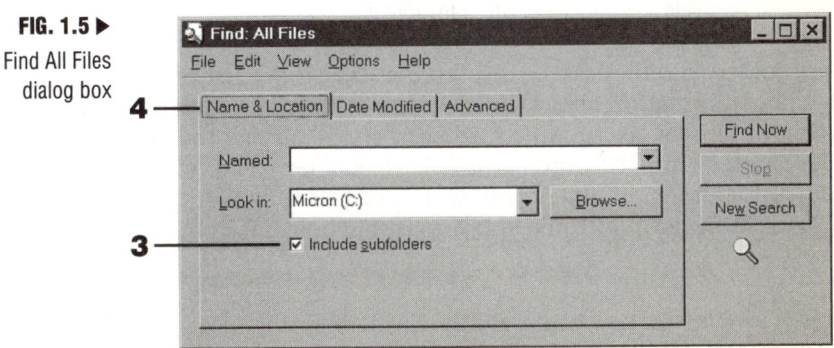

5

Managing Files
New Options in the Save As Dialog Box

You use the Save As dialog box to save a file for the first time, save a copy of the active file under another name, and save a copy of the active file in a different location.

When you save a file for the first time or select the File, Save As command, the Save As dialog box appears. You then indicate the filename, file type, and location where the file should be saved. Additionally, you have several options for protecting the file with a password. The figures to the right show the Save As dialog boxes for Office 4.3 (Figure 1.6) and Office 97 (Figure 1.7). The Office 95 and Office 97 Save As dialog boxes are identical.

In the Office 4.3 Save As dialog box, the default file location is the directory (folder) in which the program is stored. For example, the Winword directory would appear as the default file location for a Word 6.0 (Word 95) document.

When you save a new file in Office 95 and Office 97, the default file location, the My Documents folder, appears. If you choose the File, Save As command to make a copy of the file, the folder in which the original file is stored appears in the Save As dialog box.

When you save a file in Office 4.3, you generally give a file a name (and if necessary choose a file type), and then indicate the file location. In the revised Save As dialog box in Office 95 and Office 97, the location is selected first and then the filename and type.

Included in the Office 97 Save As dialog box is a series of icons for changing the location in which the file will be stored. You can **1** choose a different location to save the file in, **2** display the next level up in your list of folders (directories), or **3** display a list of folders and files you frequently access, also known as your "favorites."

> **NOTE** A new and very useful feature in the Office 95/97 Save As dialog box allows you to **4** create a new folder in which to store your file.

Your folders and files can be displayed as **5** a simple list of files, or as **6** a list with detailed information about the files such as the name, size, type, and date the folder or file was last modified. You can also **7** display the Properties of a selected file. The **8** Commands and Settings icon enables you to view the properties of a file, sort your list of folders or files, and map to a network drive. Just as in Office 4.3, the **9** Options button displays a list of choices for protecting your file.

New and Enhanced Microsoft Office Features Common to All Programs

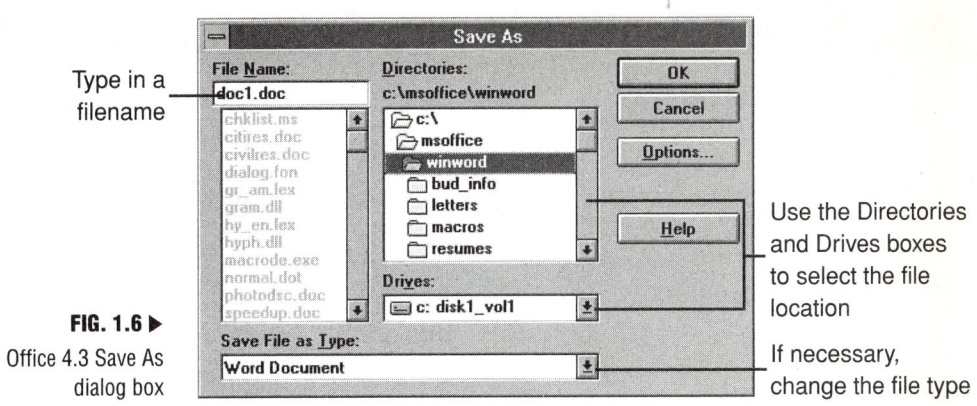

FIG. 1.6 ▶
Office 4.3 Save As dialog box

Type in a filename

Use the Directories and Drives boxes to select the file location

If necessary, change the file type

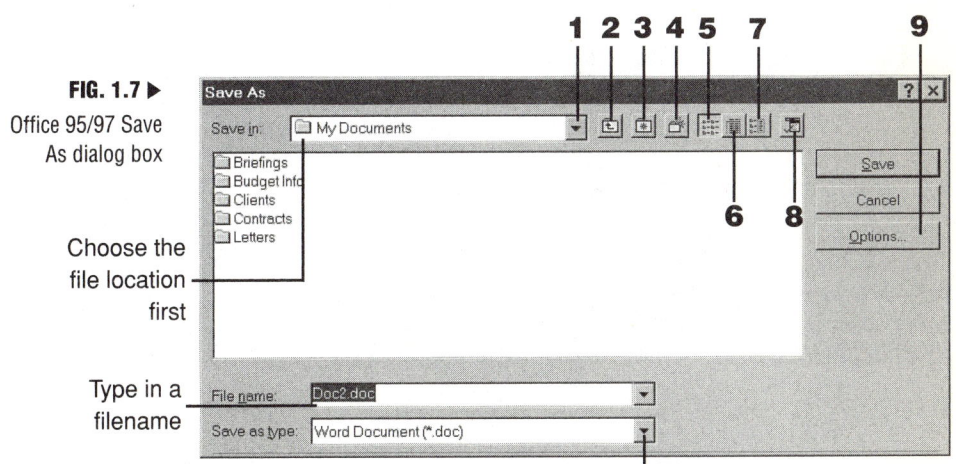

FIG. 1.7 ▶
Office 95/97 Save As dialog box

Choose the file location first

Type in a filename

If necessary, change the file type

7

Editing and Drawing Enhancements

AutoCorrect Feature Is Now Available in All Office Programs

In Office 4.3, Microsoft Word is the only program that includes the AutoCorrect feature. While in Office 95 and Office 97, all programs contain this beneficial command. This feature automatically corrects words that users frequently mistype or misspell. New words have been added to the AutoCorrect list with each new version of Microsoft Office.

Additionally, AutoCorrect will correct any capitalization it perceives to be incorrect, such as capitalizing the first two letters of a word, failure to capitalize the first letter of a sentence, and so on.

AutoCorrect is also useful when you have a lengthy word or phrase you frequently type. You can add an abbreviation that corresponds to the word or phrase to AutoCorrect. When you type the abbreviation, AutoCorrect substitutes the complete word or phrase for the abbreviation. Following are a few examples:

Abbreviation	Complete Word or Phrase
ms	Microsoft
nc	North Carolina
afb	Air Force Base

NOTE You find AutoCorrect under the Tools menu.

Figure 1.8 shows the AutoCorrect dialog box from Word 6.0, in Office 4.3.

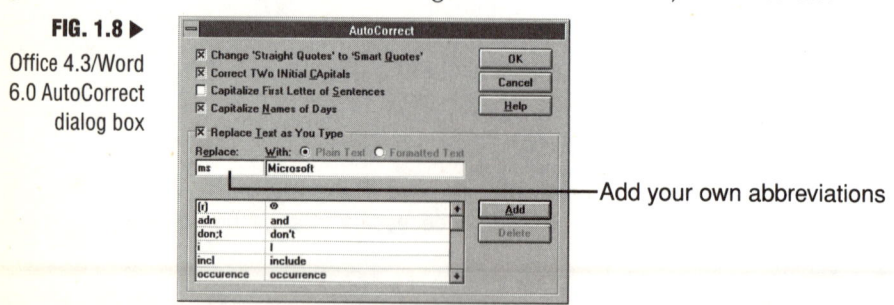

FIG. 1.8 ▶
Office 4.3/Word 6.0 AutoCorrect dialog box

Add your own abbreviations

The features are virtually identical in the Word 7.0 (Office 95) AutoCorrect dialog box, shown in Figure 1.9. The other Office 95 programs have a dialog box similar to this one. Figure 1.10 shows the AutoCorrect dialog box in Excel 97. Figure 1.11 shows the Microsoft Word 97 AutoCorrect dialog box, which is slightly different from the other Office programs.

New and Enhanced Microsoft Office Features Common to All Programs

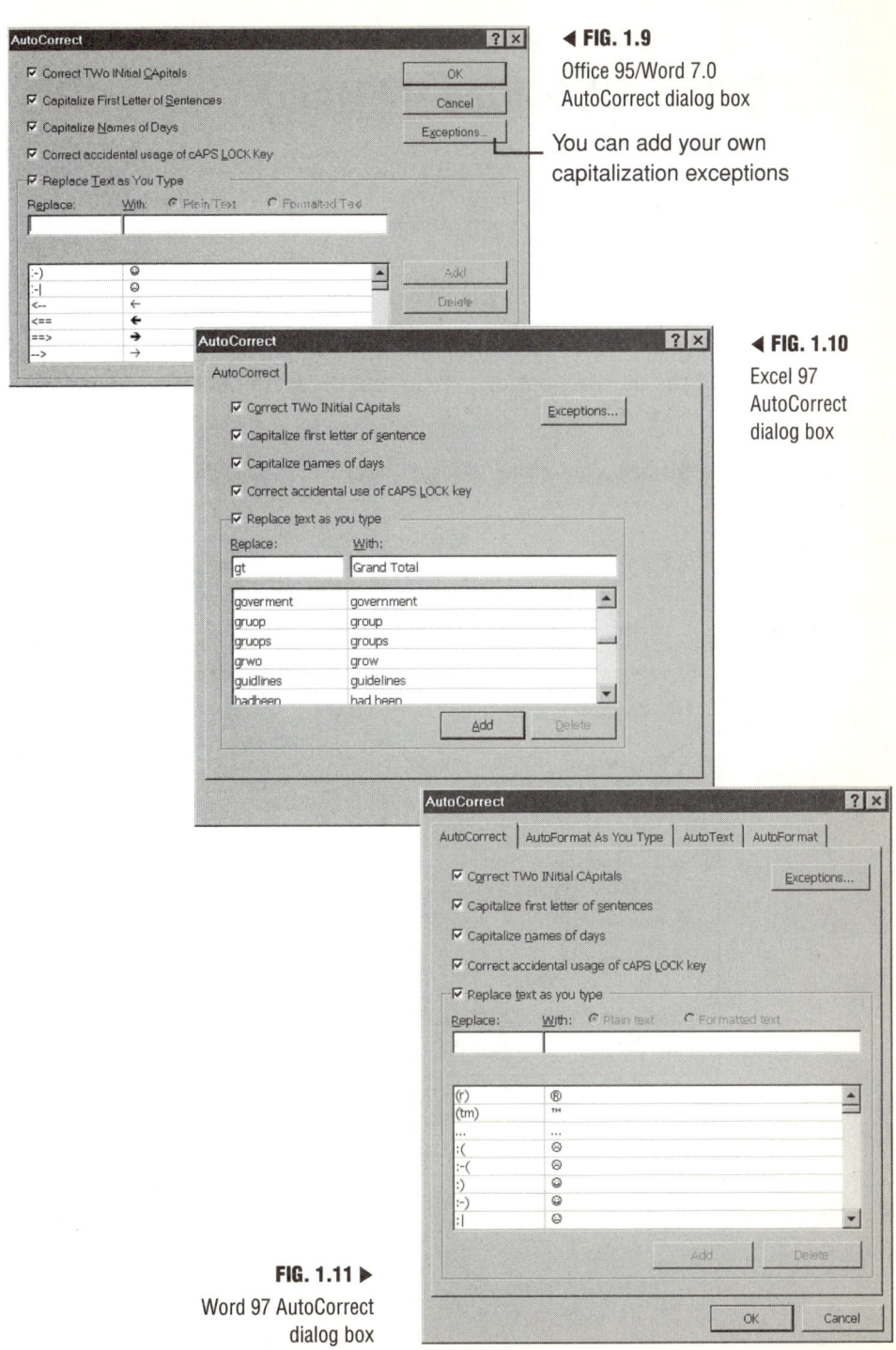

◄ FIG. 1.9
Office 95/Word 7.0
AutoCorrect dialog box

You can add your own capitalization exceptions

◄ FIG. 1.10
Excel 97
AutoCorrect
dialog box

FIG. 1.11 ►
Word 97 AutoCorrect
dialog box

Editing and Drawing Enhancements
Using Office Art (Office 97 Only)

An exciting new feature in all Office 97 programs is called Office Art. Expanding on the WordArt feature, you can now add WordArt, three-dimensional objects, and other shapes and drawn objects to your Office 97 files. WordArt is not available to other versions of Office.

To access this feature, simply display the Drawing toolbar in any program. Figure 1.12 shows the Drawing toolbar along with some of the objects you can add to your files. **1** WordArt has been integrated into this toolbar. Figures 1.13, 1.14, and 1.15 show some of the drawing options, including the **2** AutoShapes, **3** Shadow, and **4** 3-D effects you can apply to objects.

> **NOTE** Select the Drawing button on the Standard toolbar to display the Drawing toolbar.

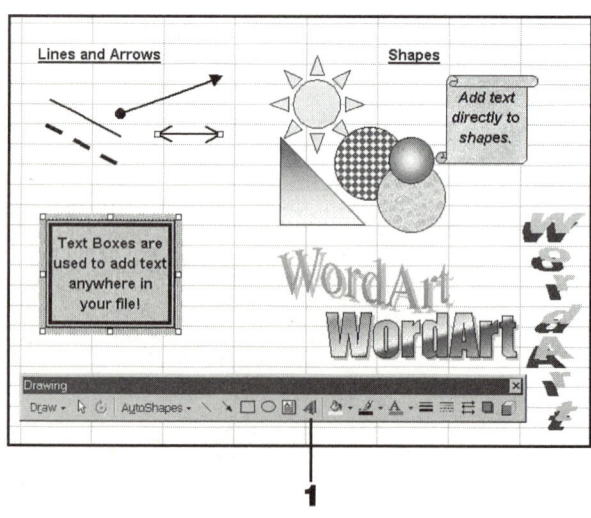

FIG. 1.12 ▶
Objects created with the Drawing toolbar

New and Enhanced Microsoft Office Features Common to All Programs

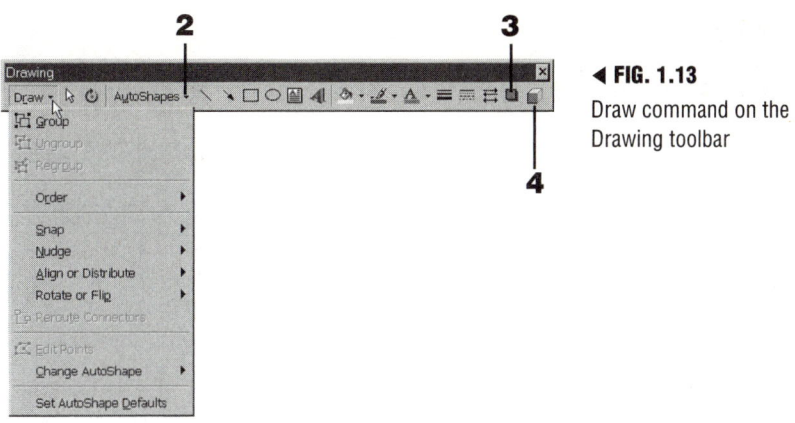

◀ **FIG. 1.13**
Draw command on the Drawing toolbar

FIG. 1.14 ▶
AutoShapes list

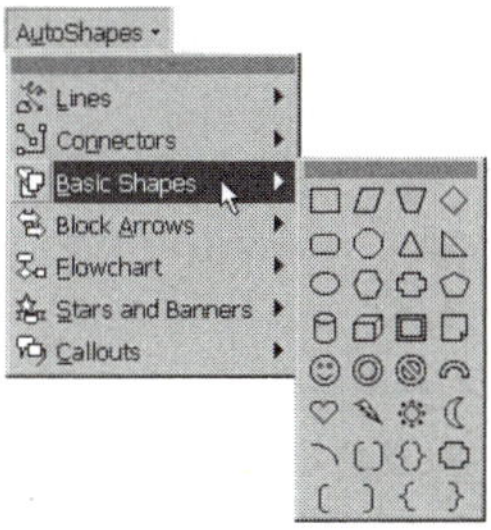

◀ **FIG. 1.15**
Apply Shadows

Expanded Online Help

Revised Table of Contents and Index Help Screens

With each new version of Office, Microsoft has improved the online help available to users. The Office 4.3 Help includes a general table of contents, as shown in Figure 1.16, and provides a search feature and index. The Office 95 and Office 97 Help Topics dialog boxes are similar. Included in the Help Topics dialog box are three tabs: Contents, Index, and Find.

Figure 1.17 shows an example of the Contents tab of the Excel 97 Help Topics dialog box. In Office 95 and Office 97, the table of contents has been revised to display a longer list of topics. Each general topic is represented by a **1** book icon. When you double-click on the book icon, a list of subtopics appears, and the symbol changes to an **2** open book icon. Specific help topics display a page icon with a **3** question mark (?), while additional subtopics display a book icon.

Figure 1.18 shows an example of the Index tab of the Excel 97 Help Topics dialog box. This feature is similar to the Search capability in Office 4.3. You enter the first few letters of the topic you need more information about, and a list of the corresponding help topics appears.

The third tab in the Help Topics dialog box accesses the Find feature. This feature enables you to locate all the help screens that contain a word or phrase in the help topic. The Find feature conducts a search of the text in the body of the help screens and displays a list of all help topics that contain the word or phrase for which you searched.

FIG. 1.16 ▶
Office 4.3 Help screen

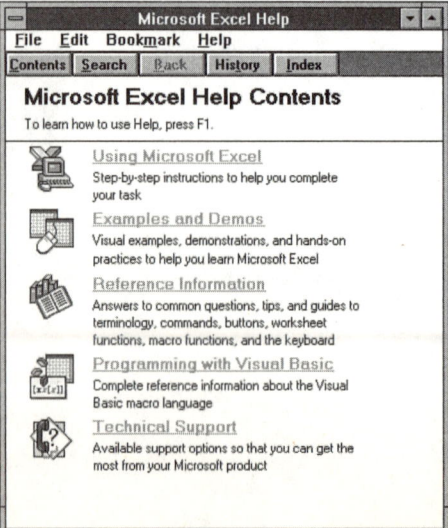

New and Enhanced Microsoft Office Features Common to All Programs

FIG. 1.17 ▶
Office 95/97 Help Topics—
Contents tab

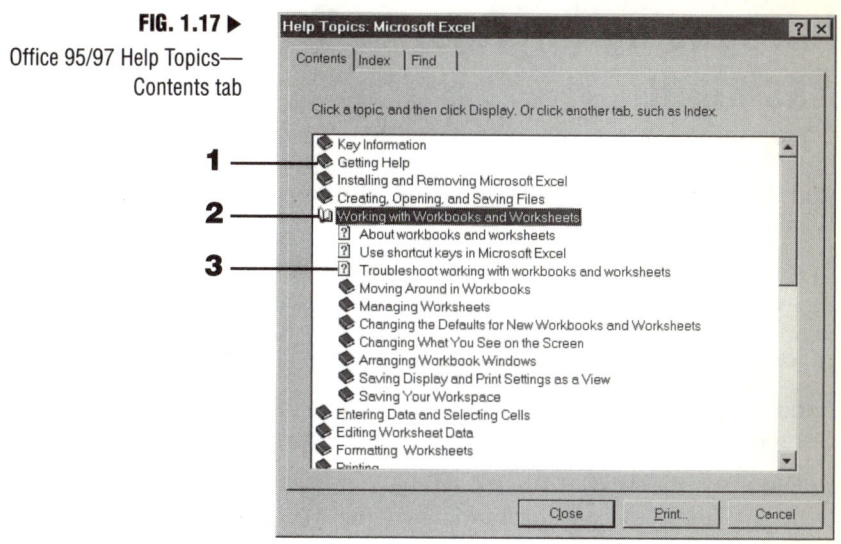

FIG. 1.18 ▶
Office 95/97 Help Topics—
Index tab

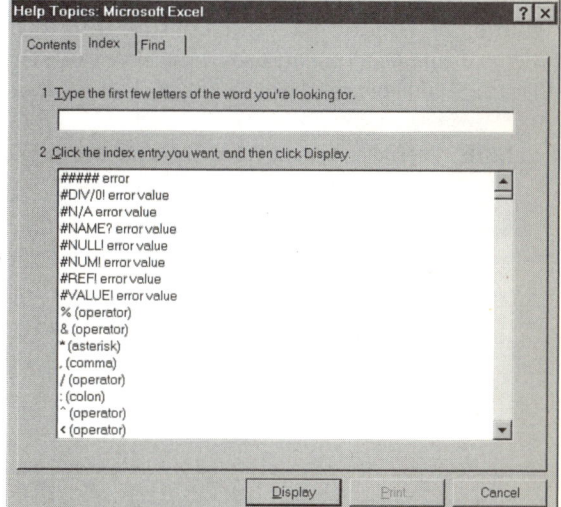

13

Expanded Online Help

Introducing the Answer Wizard and Office Assistant

In Office 95, a new feature has been added to the online help, making it easier to find information about your programs. This new help feature is the Answer Wizard, shown in Figure 1.19.

In step 1, you type in your question. Figure 1.19 shows how you can use the Answer Wizard to seek help with creating a database. In step 2, a list of topics relating to creating databases appears. Some of the help topics provide step-by-step procedures, and others display sample screens with interactive help.

Additionally, you continue to have the option of locating help topics through the Contents, Index, and Find tabs in the Help Topics dialog box.

In Office 97, the Answer Wizard has been replaced with the Office Assistant. The Office Assistant appears automatically when you first open an Office 97 program. At first you might be uncomfortable with the appearance of the Assistant; however, you will soon discover how useful it can be!

You can resize or close the Office Assistant if you prefer not to receive assistance, or if the Office Assistant obstructs your viewing your files. To display the Office Assistant again, use the button on the toolbar or press F1.

The default image used for the Office Assistant is a paper clip called "Clippit" (see Figure 1.20). Use the **1** Options button in the Office Assistant pop-up to display a gallery of images you can use, including ones that look like Albert Einstein, William Shakespeare, a dog, a cat, a spacecraft, a bouncing dot, and earth.

> **NOTE** Depending on how Office 97 was loaded on your machine, you may need the Office 97 CD to change the Office Assistant image.

New and Enhanced Microsoft Office Features Common to All Programs

FIG. 1.19 ▶

Office 95 Answer Wizard

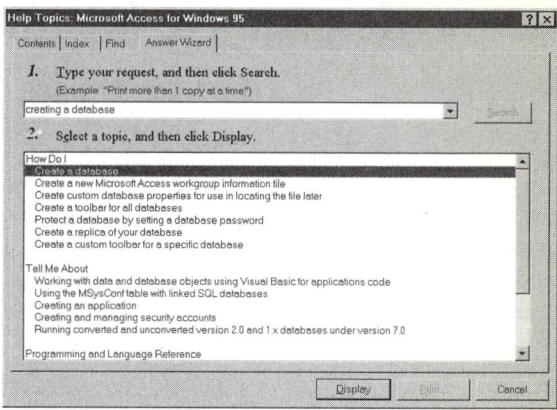

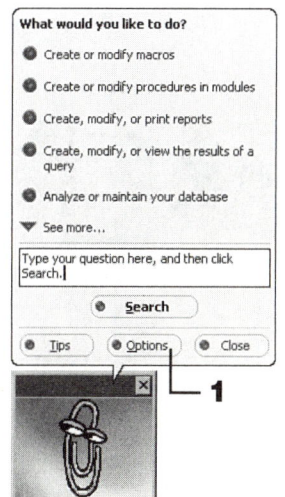

◀ **FIG. 1.20**

Office Assistant in Office 97

15

Expanded Online Help
Online Help via the Internet (Office 97 Only)

Microsoft has dedicated a large number of Web pages to provide additional information about its software programs. One of the most useful features in Office 97 is the capability to access this information directly from the Help menu. Figure 1.21 shows a typical Office 97 Help menu with the list of topics on which you can get help. The first few topics are always devoted to the program in which you are working. Figure 1.21 shows how you can get **1** free software, **2** information about upcoming changes or additions to the program, **3** answers to questions many users ask about the program, and **4** support from the Microsoft staff and power users of the software.

In addition, Microsoft provides Internet users with a **5** tutorial on using the Web, a list of the best Web sites, and a search capability.

Figure 1.22 shows the result of selecting Product News from the list of help topics.

> **NOTE** You must have access to the Internet and a Web browser program, such as Netscape Navigator or Internet Explorer, to use the Microsoft on the Web help.

FIG. 1.21 ▶
The Office 97 Help menu

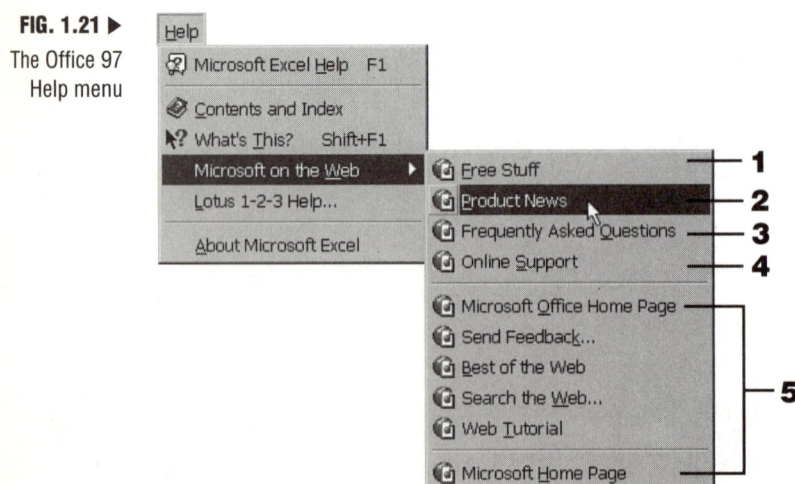

16

New and Enhanced Microsoft Office Features Common to All Programs

FIG. 1.22 ▶

An example of the Product News Web page for Microsoft Excel

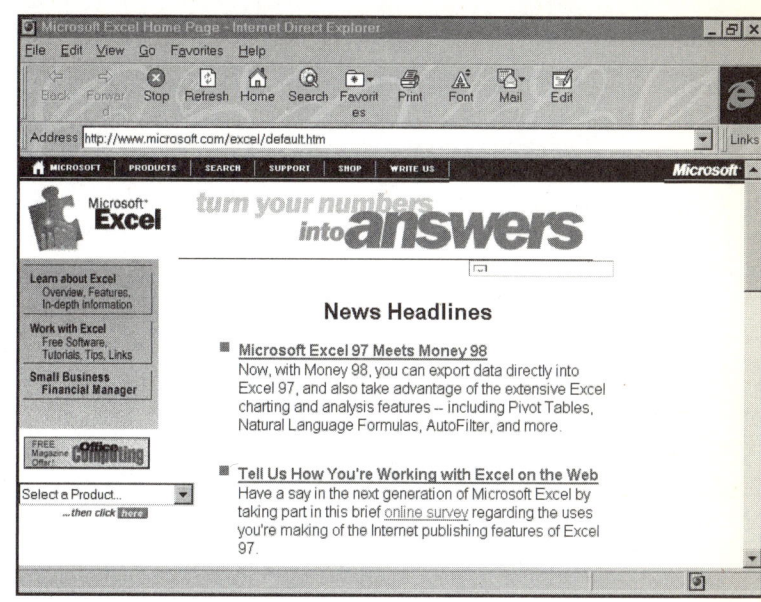

2

Upgrading to Microsoft Word 95 and Word 97

IF YOU ARE MIGRATING FROM Office 4.3 to Office 95 or Office 97, you will be pleased with the new and enhanced features that have been added to Word. The features introduced in this chapter are grouped by topic:

- **What's New.** Learn about the new features that have been added to Word.
- **Managing Files.** Convert the files you created in previous versions of Word to your current version of Word. Use the built-in templates to quickly create resumes, newsletters, legal pleadings, Web pages, brochures, memos, and awards. Save your Word files in HTML format so that they can be used as Web pages.
- **Editing Text.** Explore the revised spelling and grammar options.
- **Tables.** See how you can use the new Table and Border toolbars and the new Draw Table command to create and modify tables. Reformat the row height and column width.
- **Templates and Forms.** Discover the new built-in templates added to Word 95 and Word 97. Create your own custom templates.
- **Font Enhancements.** Improve your documents with the new font enhancements.
- **Tracking Revisions.** Tracking changes to a document has never been easier than with the new workgroup features.

Keep on top of *exactly* who made each change with the expanded revision marks. View comments added by colleagues. Merge several copies of a document into on document to see all changes and comments. Compare the original text to the revised text quickly.

What's New
Word 95

Word 95 contains a number of new or enhanced features. The following list describes many of these new features:

- **AutoFormat As You Type.** As you type, you can apply specific types of formatting to your document. You can format borders, headings, ordinal numbers, fractions, numbered lists, and bulleted lists. You activate this feature through the Tools, Option command. Select the AutoFormat tab in the Options dialog box to select from the list of formatting choices.
- **Editing Email.** If you use Microsoft Exchange/Schedule+ for email, you can use Word to create and edit email messages.
- **Highlighting Text.** Places a colored background behind text. Especially useful if you are sharing documents with colleagues and want to "flag" text you have changed. There is a new tool on the Formatting toolbar for highlighting text.
- **Templates.** Templates are now easier to locate and use. Three distinct styles have been created for templates: professional, contemporary, and elegant. Some templates use wizards to assist you in creating documents.
- **Tip Wizard.** This feature tracks your actions and makes suggestions on easier ways to accomplish the same action. The Tip Wizard is represented by a button with a lightbulb image on the Standard toolbar. Replaces Tip of the Day.
- **Spelling Indicator.** When you type in text that may be misspelled, a red wavy line appears under the word. This provides you with an immediate indication that Word does not recognize your text.

   NOTE   To see examples of the new features in Word 95, use the Answer Wizard. Type in **what's new** in the Answer Wizard search box and press Enter. Select What's New in Microsoft Word 95 from the list of help topics.

Word 97

Word 97 includes all the enhancements listed under the Word 95 section, as well as some additional features. The following list describes the most significant of these new features:

- **AutoComplete.** When you type in common entries (dates, names of the month or week, salutations and closings, mailing instructions), Word

Upgrading to Microsoft Word 95 and Word 97

automatically displays the full text. You accept the text by pressing Enter. Choose Insert, AutoText for a list of categories of common entries Word can complete. Select AutoText to see an alphabetical list of all entries.

- **AutoSummarize.** The main points in a lengthy document are identified, and a summary is generated. Choose Tools, AutoSummarize to see a list of options you can choose from.
- **Formatting Additions.** Several new effects have been added to enhance text, including shadows, outlines, and engraving. You can also animate text so it blinks, shimmers, or sparkles. Borders can be added to the current page or every page in the document and are visible in the Page Layout view.
- **Internet and Intranet Features.** You can save your Word document in an HTML format (used for Web pages), apply color or texture to the background, use the new Online Layout view (which contains a feature called Document Map) to display the main components of a document, or create a *hyperlink* (a pointer) from one document to another, including Internet Web pages.
- **Table Enhancements.** You can draw a table and use the Table and Borders toolbar to quickly format it. This version of Word also enables you to evenly distribute the rows and columns in a table and change the orientation of the text.
- **Virus Alert.** Opening a file in Office 97 that contains a macro triggers an alert message warning you that the file contains a macro and that macros may contain viruses. Because most computer viruses are macros, this message is particularly useful when opening files from other users.
- **Versions.** Word 97 enables you to save versions of the document in the same file rather than saving each version as a separate document. This command is available under the File menu.
- **Visual Basic.** Replaces WordBasic for creating macros. Macros created in WordBasic can be converted to Visual Basic.

There are some additional enhancements and minor changes in Word 97:

- New templates and wizards are available.
- You can add shading to text and borders around paragraphs.
- There are more choices for formatting numbered and bulleted lists.
- The Find, Replace, and GoTo commands have been consolidated.
- The Tip Wizard has been removed in favor of the Office Assistant.

> **NOTE** Some features from previous versions have been renamed, and some of the commands have been moved to other menus in Word 97. See a list at the end of this chapter for command menu changes.

Managing Files

Exchanging Files Between Different Versions of Word

You can display a file created in an earlier version of Word by simply opening the file in your current version of Word. For example, if you have a file created in Word 6.0 and you are currently using Word 97, open the Word 6.0 file in Word 97 to display it.

To convert a file from an earlier version of Word to a newer version, you must save the file. If you are using Word 95, when you save the file, it is immediately converted into a Word 95 format. In Word 97, when you attempt to save a file created in an earlier version of Word, the dialog box displayed in Figure 2.1 appears. You have the choice of saving the file as a Word 97 file or keeping it as a Word 6.0/95 file.

When you create a file in Word 95, you do not have to save the file in a Word 6.0 format to open the file in Word 6.0. Any formatting features in Word 95, such as highlighting text, will not be displayed in Word 6.0. If the file is changed in Word 6.0, any formatting features specific to Word 95 will be lost.

When you create a file in Word 97, you must save the file in a Word 6.0/95 format if you want to open the file in these versions of Word. Figure 2.2 shows an example of a Word 97 file being saved in a Word 6.0/95 format. Any formatting features specific to Word 97 will not be saved with the file.

When Word 97 was first released, documents saved in a Word 6.0/95 format were saved as Rich Text Format (.rtf) files. Additionally, users were noticing a significant increase in file size when they saved Word 97 files into Word 6.0/95 format, due to the compression features in Word 97. Today, Microsoft's Web site contains a revised converter file that fixes these problems.

To download this converter, you must have access to the Internet. In Word 97, choose Help, Microsoft on the Web, and select Free Stuff. When the Microsoft Free Stuff screen appears, scroll down in the list until you see **Word 6.0/95 Binary Converter for Word 97**, as shown in Figure 2.3. Choose the **1** More Info link to see an explanation of what this converter will do.

> **TIP** Ask the Office Assistant how to convert several files to Word 97 at one time.

Upgrading to Microsoft Word 95 and Word 97

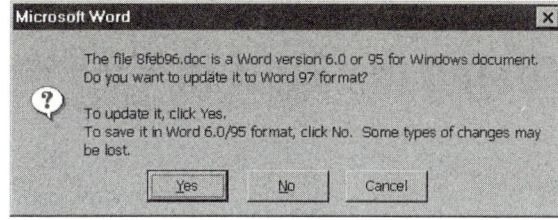

◀ **FIG. 2.1**
Word 97 update dialog box

FIG. 2.2 ▶
Word 97 Save As dialog box

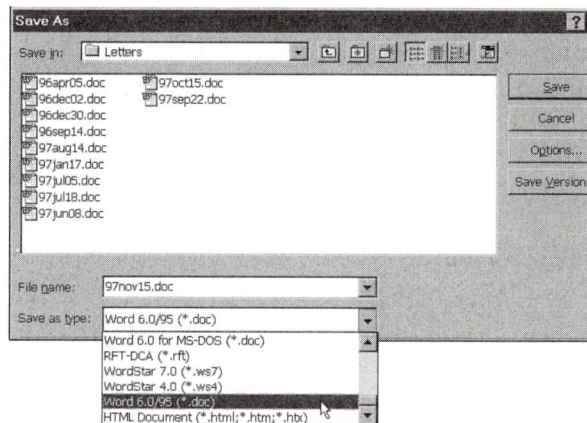

FIG. 2.3 ▶
Download the Word 6.0/95 Converter

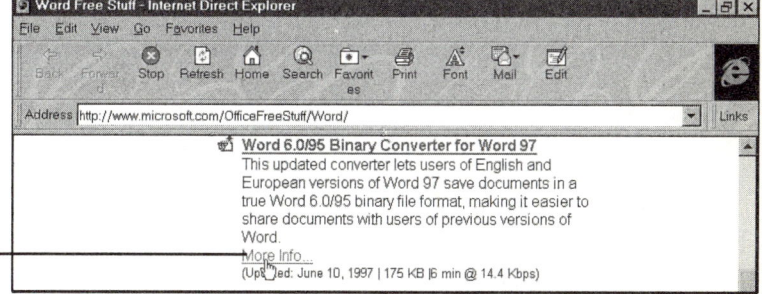

23

Managing Files

Creating New Files Using the Built-in Templates

When you choose the File, New command in Word 95 and Word 97, you discover a wide range of built-in templates that hardly resemble the templates found in Word 6.0. The former templates have been updated to depict professional, contemporary, and elegant styles. Many of the new templates use wizards, which prompt you for information in order to create the document.

As you can see in Figures 2.4 and 2.5, the templates are now divided into distinct categories, making it much easier to locate templates more quickly.

Figure 2.4 shows the New dialog box in Word 95. The Award Wizard template on the Other Documents tab has been selected. A preview of the document appears on the right side of the dialog box.

Figure 2.5 shows the New dialog box in Word 97. The Contemporary Report has been selected from the Reports tab, and a preview of the report appears on the right side of the dialog box. One of the tabs in this figure lists the Office 95 templates. This tab appears only if Word 95 was on your machine when Word 97 was installed.

Many of the templates can be previewed, allowing you to see an overall depiction of the document before you create it. However, a few templates cannot be previewed, most notably the Web Pages templates.

> **NOTE** If you use the New button on the Standard toolbar to create a new document, the Blank Document template is automatically used to create the file. You must use the File, New command to see a list of the built-in templates.

> **TIP** If you have access to the Internet, you can use the Help, Microsoft on the Web, Free Stuff command to look for additional templates available from Microsoft.

Upgrading to Microsoft Word 95 and Word 97

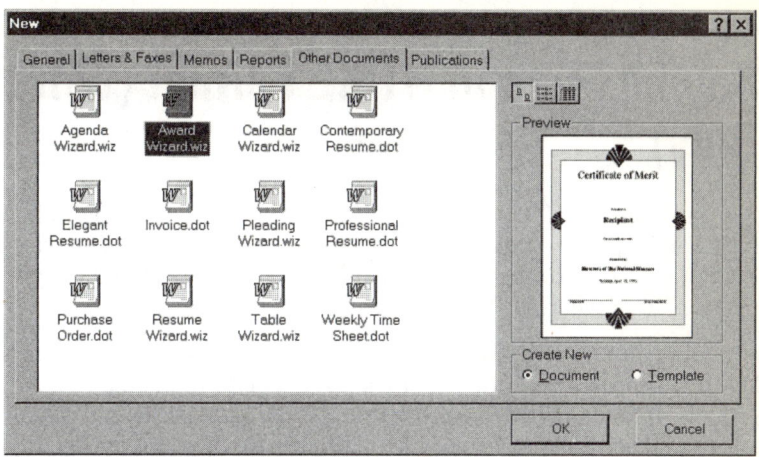

FIG. 2.4 ▶
Word 95 New dialog box

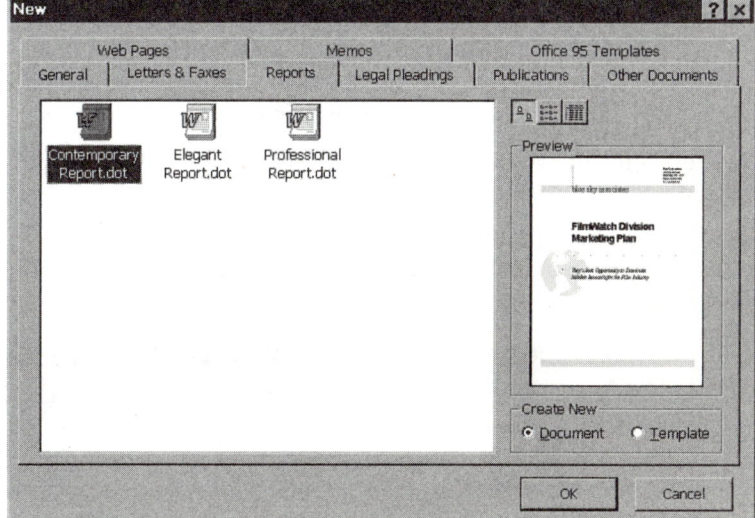

◀ **FIG. 2.5**
Word 97 New dialog box

Managing Files

Saving Files in HTML Format (Word 97 Only)

You can save Word 97 files in the *Hypertext Markup Language (HTML)* format. This format is required for files that will be Web pages on the Internet World Wide Web or on your company's internal intranet. To save a file in the HTML format, choose File, Save as HTML.

As with other files, you need to supply a **1** location and **2** name for this file. Figure 2.6 shows an example of the Save As HTML dialog box. As part of the process to convert the Word file into HTML format, several dialog boxes may appear. Figure 2.7 shows one of the dialog boxes you may see. It warns you to save the file before converting to HTML because some formats may be lost as a result of the conversion.

Because Microsoft periodically makes new Web page authoring tools available, you may be asked if you want to connect to the Internet to check to see whether there is a new version of the Web page authoring tools. This will be followed by a prompt asking whether you want to access the Microsoft Web site to download a new version of these tools. Figures 2.8 and 2.9 show examples of these prompts.

Figure 2.10 displays the Microsoft Web page that provides a **3** status of the latest Web page authoring tools for Word 97.

After a Word 97 file has been converted to HTML, it appears differently on the screen. The toolbar buttons and menu commands are changed to provide tools to format and edit the HTML file.

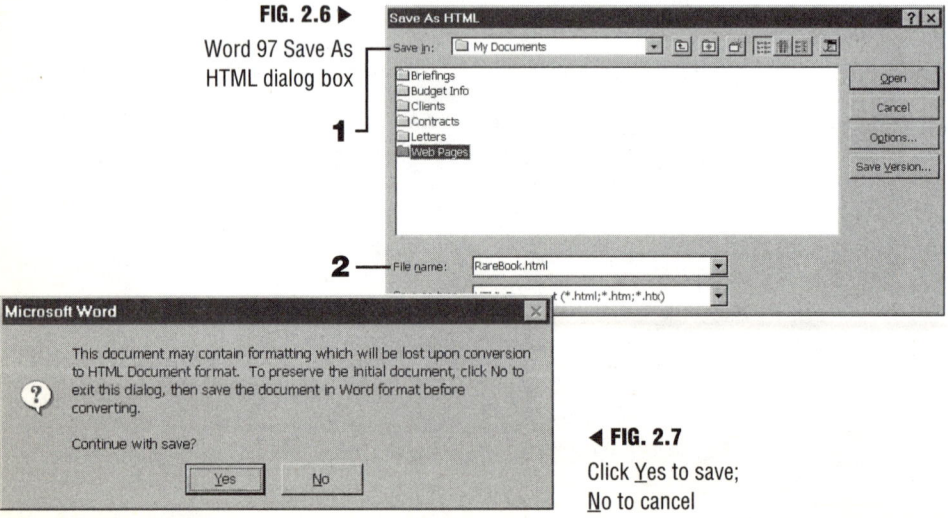

FIG. 2.6 ▶
Word 97 Save As HTML dialog box

◀ **FIG. 2.7**
Click Yes to save;
No to cancel

Upgrading to Microsoft Word 95 and Word 97

◄ **FIG. 2.8**
Downloading Web page authoring tools

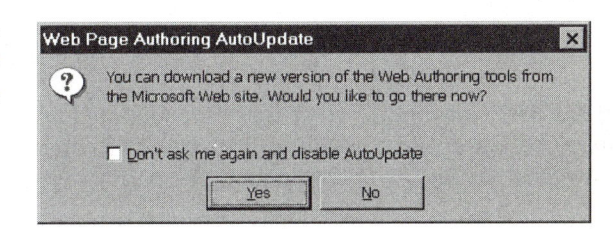

FIG. 2.9 ►
Word 97 AutoUpdate

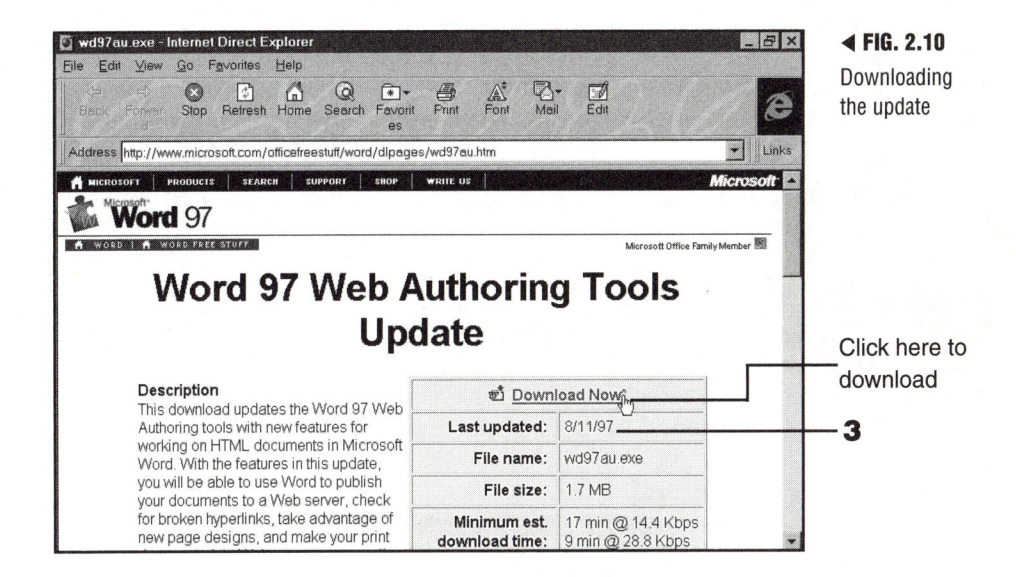

◄ **FIG. 2.10**
Downloading the update

Click here to download

3

Editing Text
Improved Spell Check and Grammar Options

Several significant additions have been made in the area of spelling and grammar in Word 95 and Word 97. When you type a word the program does not recognize, a red wavy line appears beneath the word. This provides you with an immediate indication that the word is located in the Microsoft Office or custom dictionaries. The word may be misspelled, a duplicate, an abbreviation, a proper name, or from a language other than English.

Additionally, Word 97 displays a wavy green line to alert you of a possible grammatical error.

In Word 6.0 and Word 95, the commands that check spelling and grammar are activated separately. As you can see in Figures 2.11 and 2.12, there is little difference in the options available in the Spelling dialog boxes of Word 6.0 and Word 95.

In Word 97, these two features have been combined into one command. Figure 2.13 shows the Spelling and Grammar dialog box in Word 97. You can set the parameters for spelling and grammar by selecting the **1** Spelling and Grammar tab in the Tools, Options dialog box, as shown on the left side of Figure 2.14 on the next page. The right side of this figure shows the grammar options you can select by clicking the **2** Settings button in the Options dialog box. You can also access the Options dialog box by choosing the Options button in the Spelling and Grammar dialog box.

In all versions of Word, the spelling and grammar commands are located under the Tools menu.

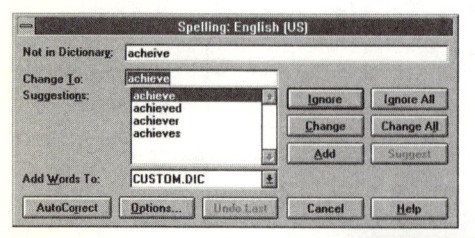

◀ **FIG. 2.11**
Word 6.0 Spelling dialog box

FIG. 2.12 ▶
Word 95 Spelling dialog box

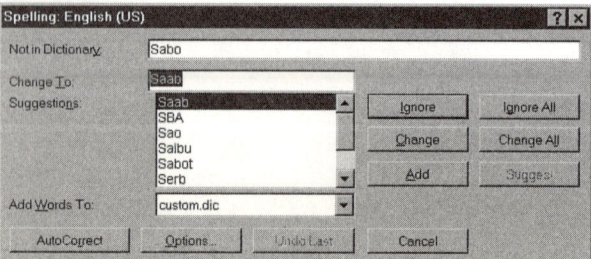

Upgrading to Microsoft Word 95 and Word 97

FIG. 2.13 ▶
Word 97 Spelling and Grammar dialog box

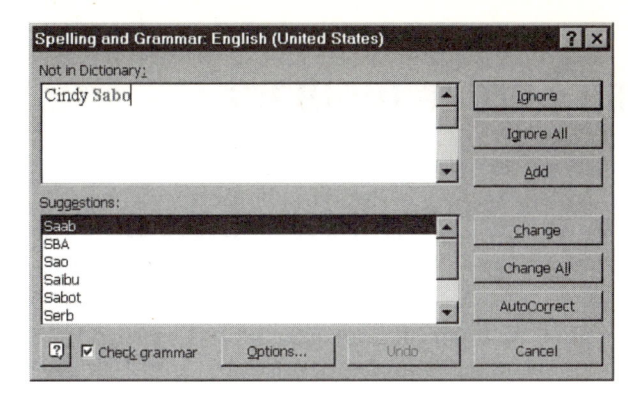

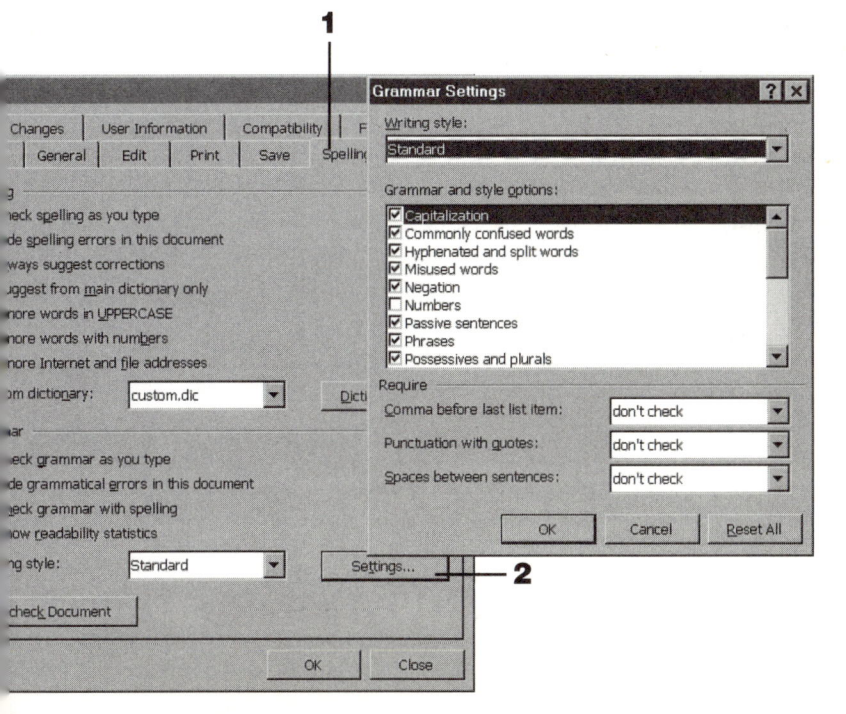

◀ FIG. 2.14
Spelling and grammar options

Tables
Table and Border Toolbars

In Word 6.0 and Word 95, a button on the Formatting toolbar activates the Borders toolbar, which is useful in applying borders to tables. Figure 2.15 shows a table in Word 6.0 with the Borders toolbar displayed below the table. On the Formatting toolbar, the mouse is pointing to the button that activates the Borders toolbar.

In Word 97, the new Tables and Borders toolbar has been added to the list of toolbars. This new toolbar includes the border features found on the Borders toolbar from Word 6.0 and Word 95 and adds common table features as well. Figure 2.16 on the next page shows a table in Word 97 with the Tables and Borders toolbar displayed below the table. On the Standard toolbar, the mouse is pointing to the button that activates this toolbar. Some of the commands available on the Tables and Borders toolbar are

- **1** Draw Table and Eraser
- **2** Line and Border Formats
- **3** Merge or Split Cells
- **4** Vertical Alignment
- **5** Distribute Rows or Columns Evenly
- **6** Table AutoFormat
- **7** Change Text Direction
- **8** Sort Ascending or Descending
- **9** AutoSum

Upgrading to Microsoft Word 95 and Word 97

FIG. 2.15 ▶
A Word 6.0 table

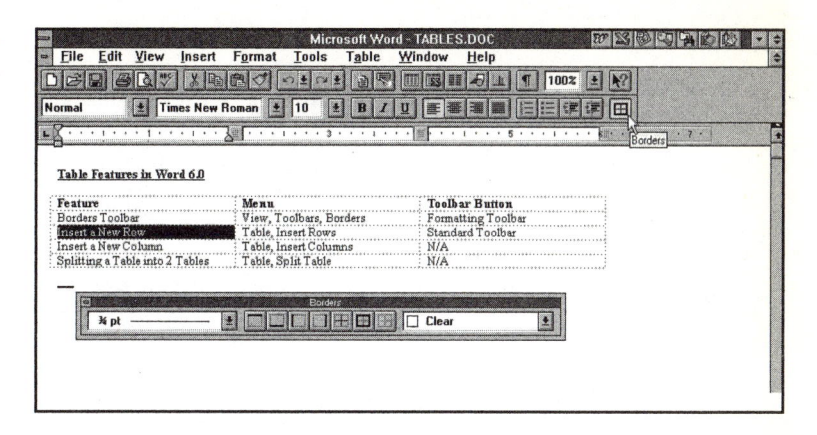

FIG. 2.16 ▶
A Word 97 table

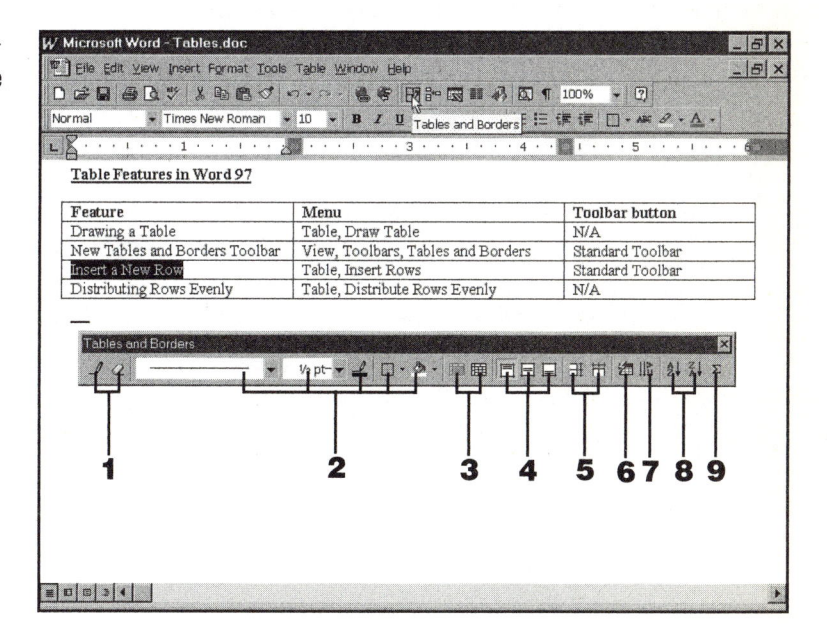

Tables
Drawing a Table (Word 97 Only)

In Word 97, you can create and format a table quickly by using the new Table, Draw Table command. By activating the new Tables and Borders toolbar, most of the table formatting options are within easy access.

> **NOTE** If you are not in the Page Layout view when you select the Draw Table command, a message appears asking whether you want to change to the Page Layout view.

The mouse pointer changes to the shape of a **1** pencil. Figure 2.17 shows the Page Layout view with the Tables and Borders toolbar.

Select the line style, weight, and color from the Tables and Borders toolbar and draw a rectangle for the outside border of the table. To create rows and columns in the table, **2** draw the horizontal and vertical lines exactly where you want them.

> **NOTE** You can use the Split Cells button to specify the rows and columns; however, this option spaces the rows and columns equally and uses the border style, weight, and color for the lines dividing the rows and columns.

Upgrading to Microsoft Word 95 and Word 97

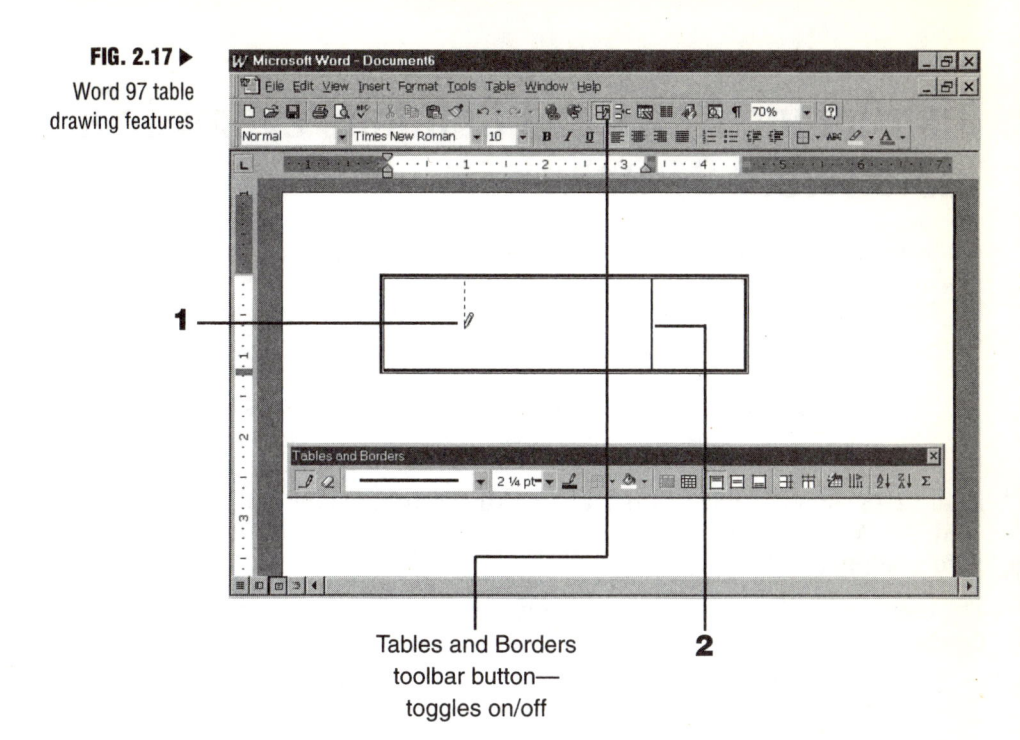

FIG. 2.17 ▶
Word 97 table drawing features

Tables and Borders toolbar button— toggles on/off

Tables

Distributing Rows and Columns Evenly in a Table (Word 97 Only)

A new feature in Word 97 is the capability to evenly space the rows and columns in a table. Formatting columns to have the same width or rows to have the same height can save time when you are trying to establish a uniform look to your tables.

> **NOTE** You can access the Distribute Columns Evenly and Distribute Rows Evenly commands from the new Tables and Borders toolbar or from the Tables menu.

Figure 2.18 shows a table before and after the Distribute Rows Evenly feature is used. The **1** Distribute Columns Evenly feature is also available on the Tables and Borders toolbar.

The text has also been centered vertically using the **2** center button on this toolbar.

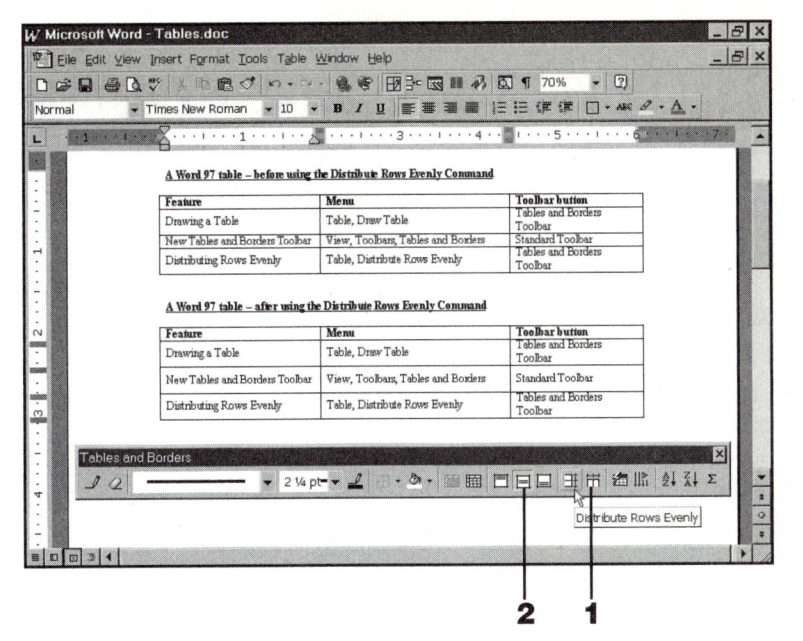

◀ **FIG. 2.18**
Word 97
Distribute Rows
Evenly feature

Tables

Changing Text Orientation in a Table (Word 97 Only)

A new feature in Word 97 is the capability to change the orientation of the text in a table. This feature has three settings: normal (left to right), top to bottom, and bottom to top. Each time you select the Change Text Direction command, it cycles through these three settings.

Figure 2.19 shows a table illustrating these three settings. The text in the middle of the table is selected. Notice the **1** Change Text Direction button on the Tables and Borders toolbar. The button image changes depending on the orientation of the selected text. Because the selected text is currently oriented top to bottom, the next direction available is bottom to top, as depicted on the button image.

Notice the **2** tools on the Formatting toolbar. Because the direction of the selected text is top to bottom, the orientation of many of the buttons has changed as well, including

- Left, Center, Right, and Justify Alignment
- Numbered and Bulleted Lists
- Decrease and Increase Indent

> **NOTE** You can access the Text Direction command either from the Format menu or through a button on the Tables and Borders toolbar. Your cursor must be inside a table for this feature to be active.

◀ **FIG. 2.19**

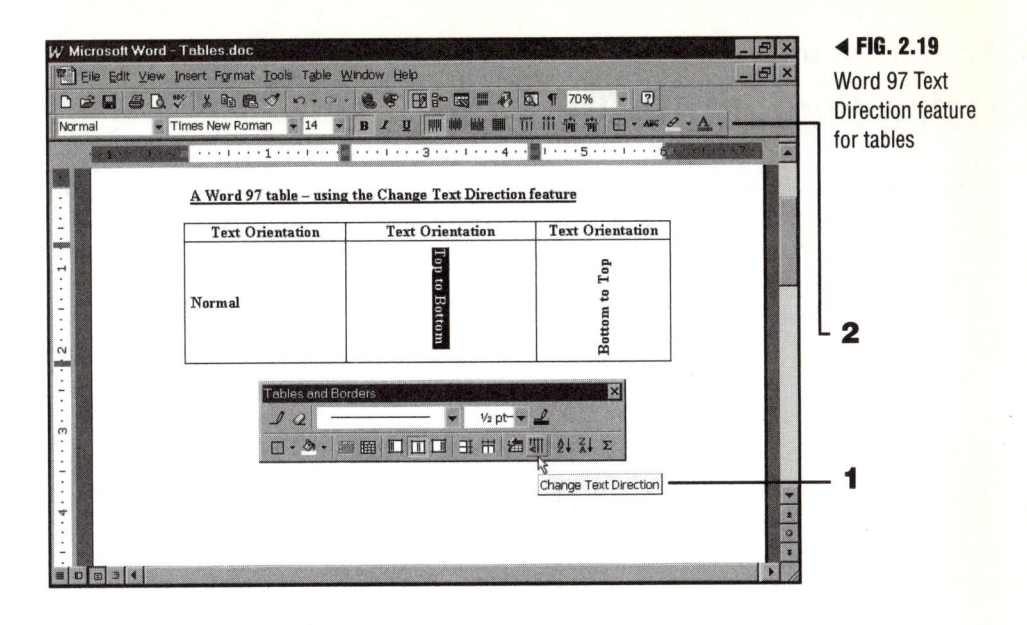

Word 97 Text Direction feature for tables

Templates and Forms
Using the Built-in Templates

Many of the templates in Word 95 and Word 97 are now designed with wizards to assist you in using the template. The wizards provide you with a list of choices for creating a document. To access the built-in templates, you must use the File, New command. Using the New button on the Standard toolbar immediately creates a blank document.

Figure 2.20 shows the New dialog box for Word 95. The list of templates is divided into categories, with **1** each category on a different tab. The Resume Wizard template on the Other Documents tab is selected. A **2** preview of the document created by a template appears on the right.

Figure 2.21 shows the first step in the Resume Wizard, asking which type of resume is to be created. A common feature of wizards is to provide an explanation or description of the selected item. In this example, the Functional resume has been created and an **3** explanation of who will benefit from this type of resume appears below the choices.

The New dialog box in Word 97 provides some **4** additional template categories, as you can see in Figure 2.22. Here, the Newsletter Wizard has been selected from the Publications tab. If you are upgrading from Office 95, the **5** templates available in Office 95 will appear on their own tab.

As you can see in Figure 2.23, the appearance of the wizards has been enhanced in Word 97. The diagram on the left of the screen depicts a **6** "road map" where you can enter the wizard at any step along the way.

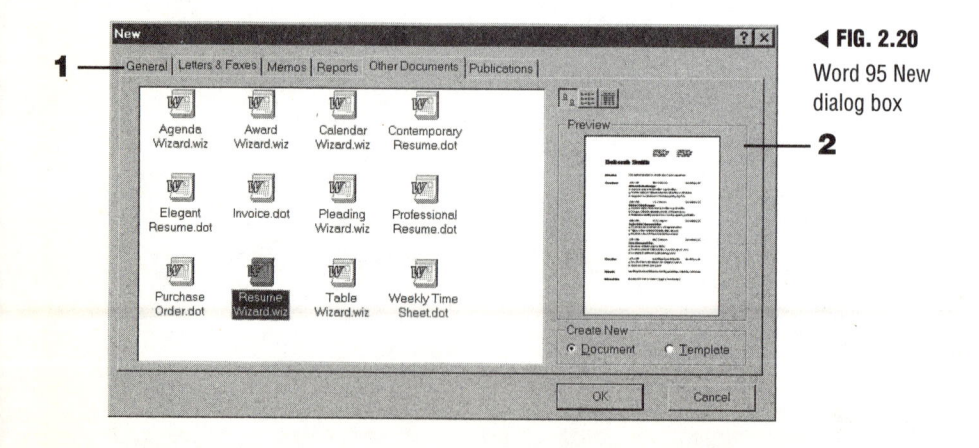

◀ **FIG. 2.20**

Word 95 New dialog box

38

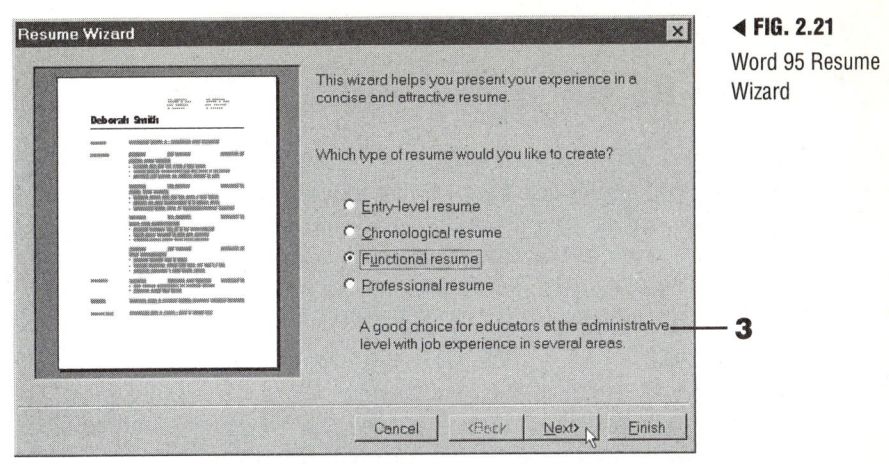

Upgrading to Microsoft Word 95 and Word 97

◀ **FIG. 2.21**
Word 95 Resume Wizard

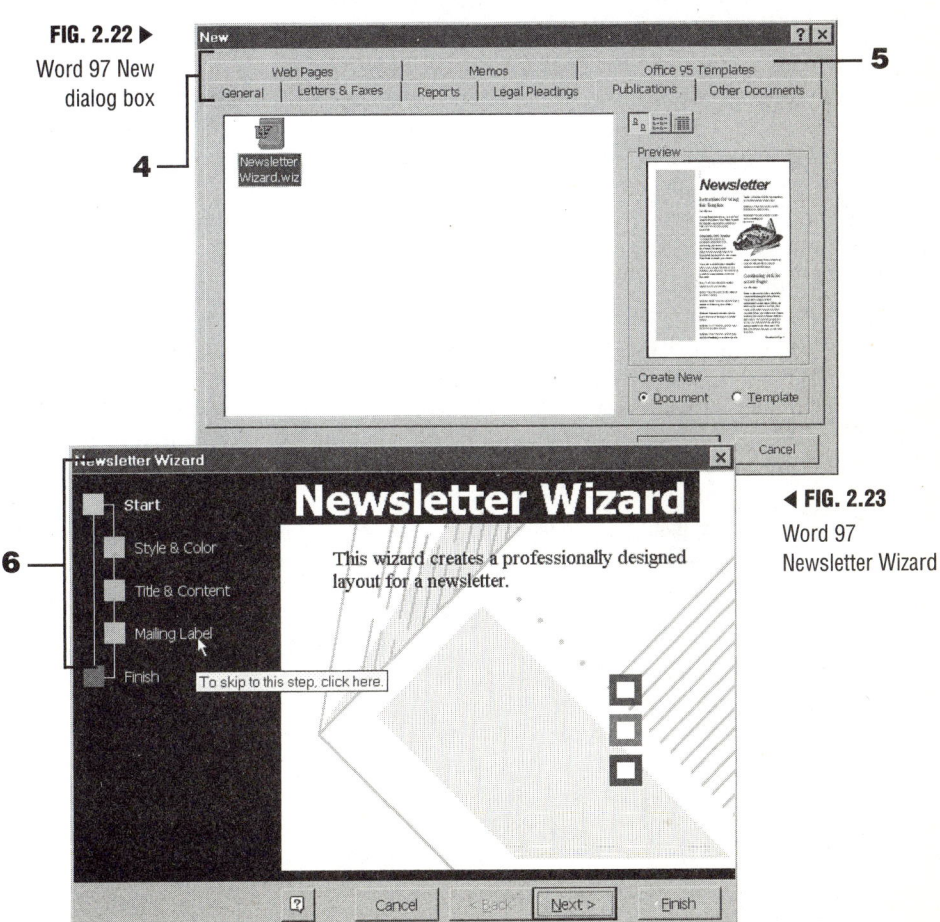

FIG. 2.22 ▶
Word 97 New dialog box

◀ **FIG. 2.23**
Word 97 Newsletter Wizard

39

Templates and Forms
Creating Custom Templates

There are three ways to create your own templates in Word: create a template from "scratch," create a template based on an existing Word document, or create a template based on an existing template. Word 6.0 (Office 4.3) enables you to create templates by using the first two methods. With the templates that are now built in to Word 95 and Word 97, it is much easier to create custom templates based on these existing professionally designed templates.

If you create a template from scratch, or base a new template on an existing document, make sure that it is the active document in Word. To create a new template based on an existing template, choose File, New and select the template you want. If the template is a wizard, proceed through the wizard to create the document. Modify the document as necessary.

After the file is created, use the File, Save As command to save it as a template file. Figure 2.24 shows the Word 97 Save As dialog box, which is nearly identical to the Word 95 Save As dialog box. In the **1** Save As Type box, choose Document Template (*.dot). Word will automatically display the Templates folder in the **2** Save In box. The folder in which you save the template determines the tab in the New dialog box, shown in Figure 2.25, where you will find the template for future use. Templates saved directly in the Templates folder in the Save As dialog box (Figure 2.24) appear on the General tab of the New dialog box (Figure 2.25). If you save a template in a subfolder of the Templates folder, such as Memos or Web Pages, the template will appear on this tab in the New dialog box. In Figure 2.24, the template named Marketing Letter is being saved in the **3** Letters & Faxes subfolder. When a new document is created using the File, New command, the New dialog box, shown in Figure 2.25, displays a list of template tabs. The template Marketing Letter is selected on the Letters & Faxes tab in Figure 2.25.

> **TIP** To learn more about creating templates, use the online help. Look up information by typing **creating templates** in the Answer Wizard in Word 95 or the Office Assistant in Word 97.

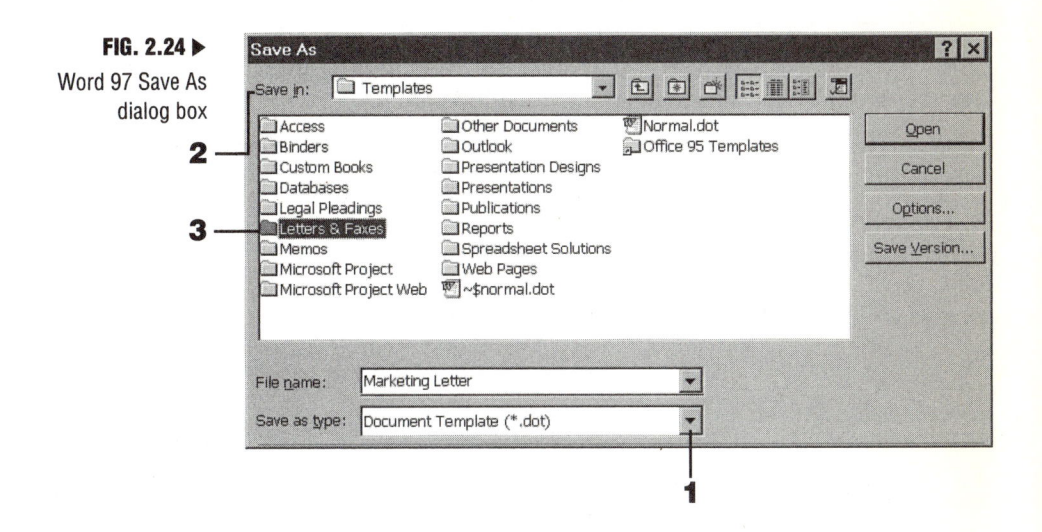

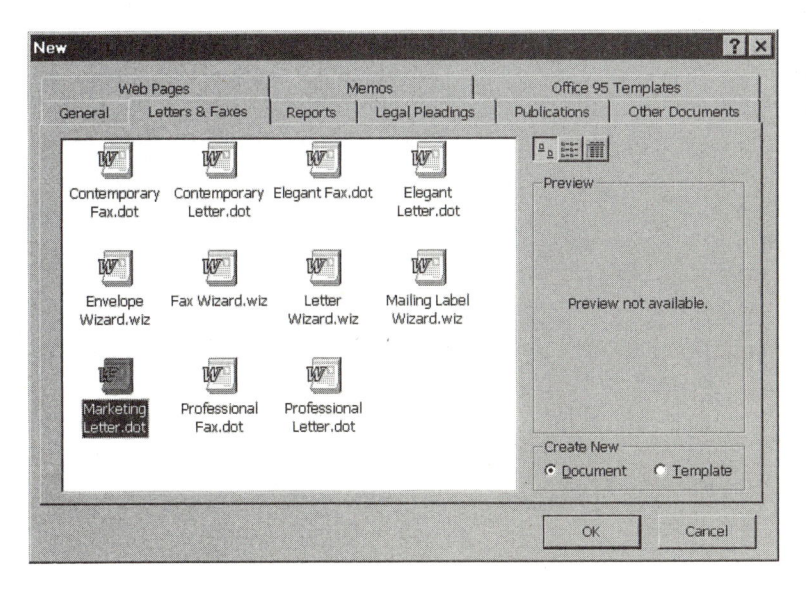

FIG. 2.24 ▶
Word 97 Save As dialog box

◀ FIG. 2.25
Word 97 New dialog box

Font Enhancements
New Font Effects (Word 97 Only)

In all versions of Word, you have the ability to apply effects to your text. Among the most common are strikethrough (abc), subscript (H_2O), and all caps (ABC). Several new font effects have been included in Word 97.

These new font effects are illustrated in Figure 2.26. The new effects are **1** double strikethrough, **2** shadow, **3** outline, **4** emboss, and **5** engrave.

To access the effects, choose Format, Font. The Font dialog box, as shown in Figure 2.26, appears. The effects are located in the middle of the first tab of this dialog box. Use the **6** preview window at the bottom of the dialog box to see how the effect will impact the appearance of your text.

Upgrading to Microsoft Word 95 and Word 97

1 — Double Strikethrough

2 — Shadow

3 — Outline

4 — Emboss

5 — Engrave

6

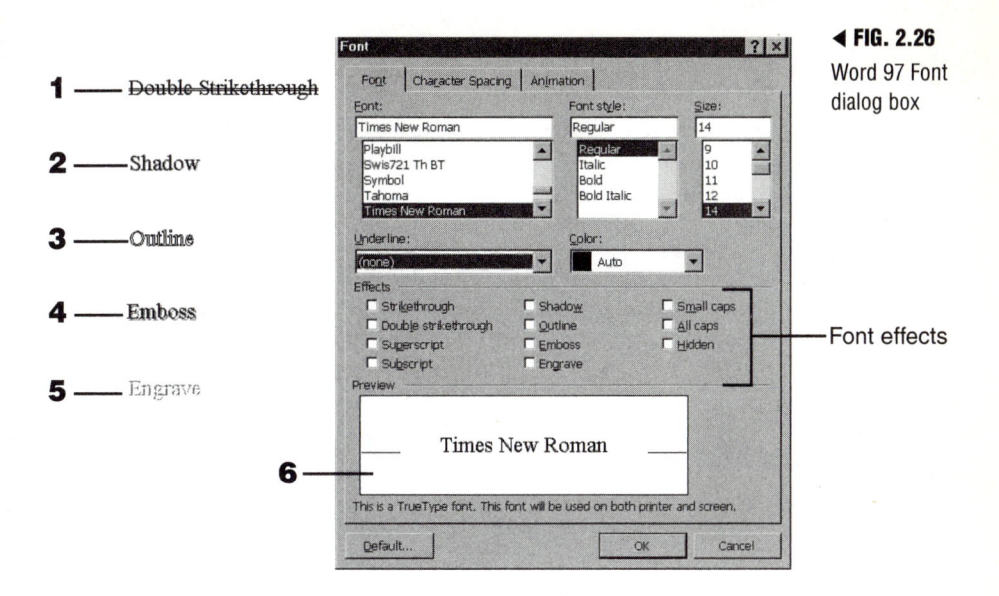

◀ **FIG. 2.26**
Word 97 Font dialog box

Font effects

Font Enhancements
Applying Font Animation (Word 97 Only)

Office 97 contains many intranet and Internet features, one of which is the capability to create documents that can be viewed online. Word 97 includes a new enhancement, which will animate text in online documents. These font effects are not available to Office 4.x and Office 95 users.

You can access these new font effects through the Font dialog box. Choose Format, Font to display this dialog box. In the Font dialog box, select the **1** Animation tab (see Figure 2.27). The new effects are listed here:

- Blinking Background
- Las Vegas Lights
- Marching Black Ants
- Marching Red Ants
- Shimmer
- Sparkle Text

Use the **2** preview window at the bottom of the dialog box to see the how the animation will impact the appearance of your text.

> **NOTE** These animation effects appear only when the document is being viewed; they do not appear when the document is printed.

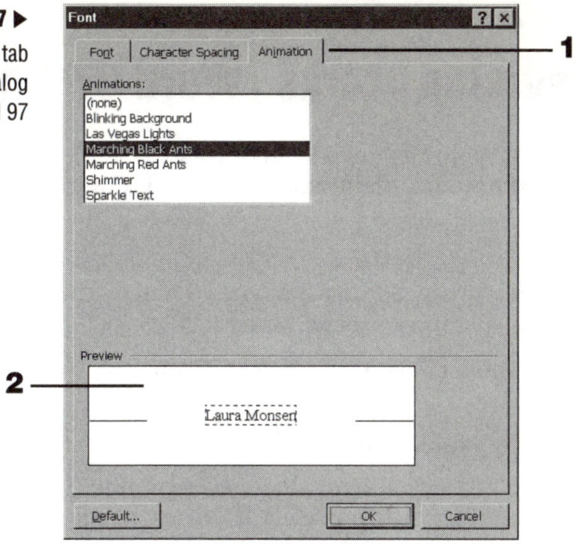

Upgrading to Microsoft Word 95 and Word 97

FIG. 2.27 ▶
The Animation tab of the Font dialog box in Word 97

Tracking Revisions

Expanded Revision Marks (Word 97 Only)

All versions of Word (4.x, 95, and 97) include an option to color code changes made to a document by other users. Additionally, **1** a vertical marker appears in the left margin to flag the line changes made, which makes it quicker to locate each change.

Word 97 expands on this feature by adding **2** a pop-up note with the user's name and the date of the change, as you can see in Figure 2.28.

The users making changes must take several steps to ensure that you can see the changes they have made:

- Open the document to be changed.
- Select Tools, Track Changes, Highlight Changes. From the Highlight Changes dialog box (see Figure 2.29), select **3** Track Changes While Editing.

    NOTE In Word 6.0 (Office 4.3) and Word 95, users should choose the Tools, Revisions command and activate the Mark Revisions While Editing option (see Figure 2.30) to display the color coded changes.

- Select Tools, Options. On the **4** User Information tab of the Options dialog box (see Figure 2.31), make sure the name of the person making the changes appears in the **5** Name box. This step is identical, regardless of the version of Word you are using.
- Make the necessary changes.

    NOTE The Track Changes While Editing feature is active only for the current document. Each time you want to show the revision marks, you will have to activate this feature.

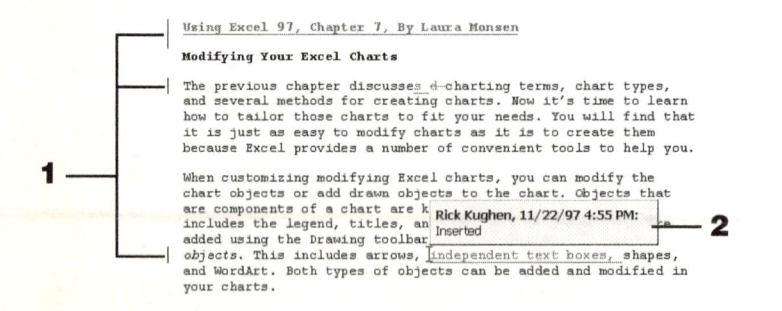

◀ **FIG. 2.28**

Word 97 enhanced revision marks

Upgrading to Microsoft Word 95 and Word 97

FIG. 2.29 ▶
Word 97 Highlight Changes dialog box

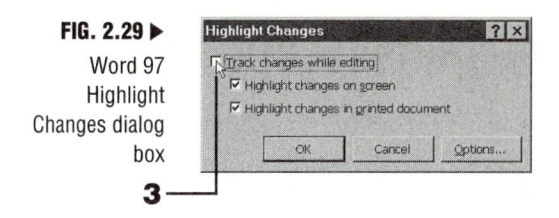

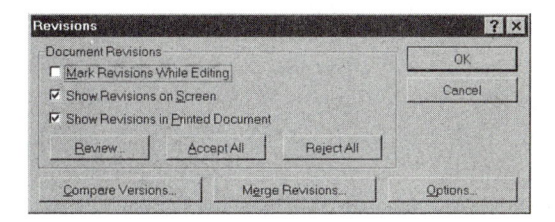

◀ FIG. 2.30
Word 6.0/95 Revisions dialog box

FIG. 2.31 ▶
Word 97 User Information tab

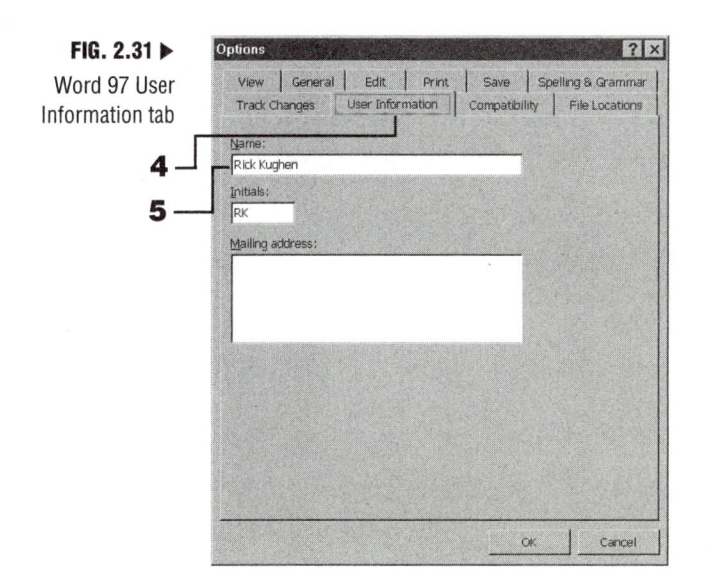

47

Tracking Revisions
Adding Comments (Word 97 Only)

In Word 6.0 (Office 4.x) and Word 95, the Annotation command is used to insert notes into documents when reviewing the text. Figure 2.32 shows an example of annotations added into a Word 6.0 document. You add and view annotations in Word 95 the same way they are added in Word 6.0.

In Word 97, this command is now called Comment. To add a comment to a document, select the text the comment will pertain to and choose Insert, Comment. Figure 2.33 shows an example of a document with several comments added. Text referred to in the comment will be **1** highlighted in pale yellow, and the **2** comments view will appear in the lower portion of the screen. The **3** initials of each person who has added comments will appear in the comments view.

In Word 97, several new features have been added to comments. The text in the document will remain highlighted in pale yellow, even when the comments view is closed. To read a comment, simply position the mouse pointer over a piece of text. The highlight will turn dark yellow, and **4** the comment will pop up on the screen.

To display the comments view again, choose View, Comments.

> **TIP** There is a new toolbar in Word 97 designed to assist in inserting and reviewing changes made to documents. Choose View, Toolbars and select Reviewing to display this toolbar. Hovering the mouse over each of the buttons will make a ScreenTip appear, describing what each button does.

Upgrading to Microsoft Word 95 and Word 97

FIG. 2.32 ▶
Annotations added to a Word 6.0/95 document

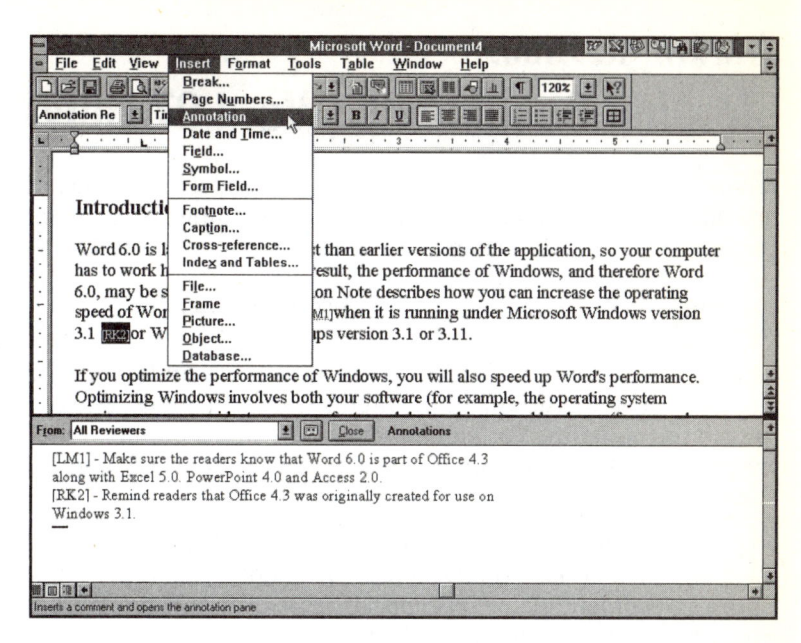

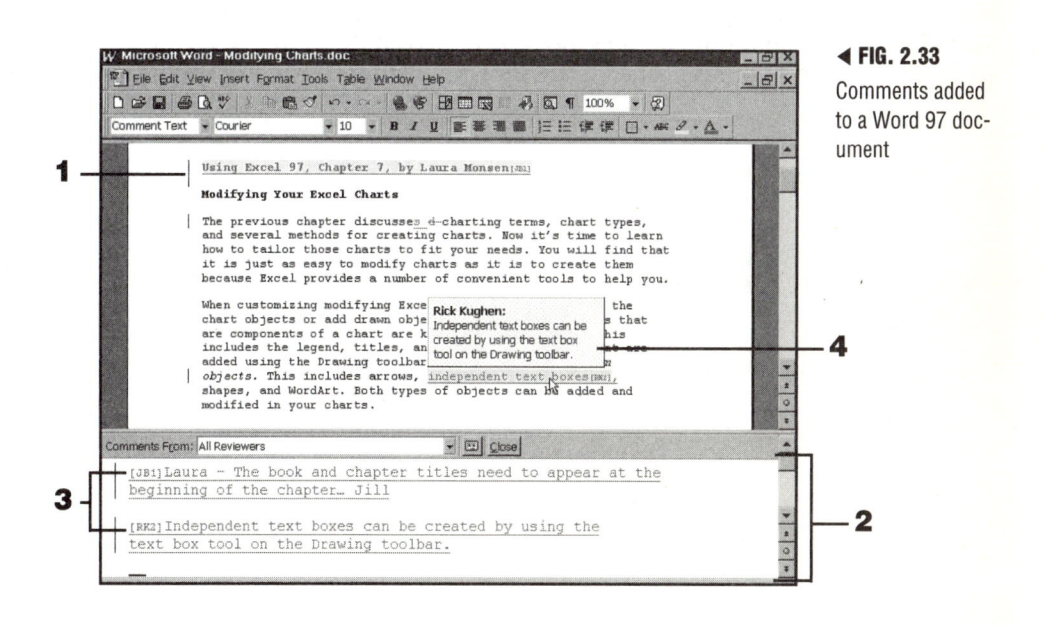

◀ FIG. 2.33
Comments added to a Word 97 document

Tracking Revisions

Merging Documents (Word 97 Only)

A new and powerful feature in Word 97 is the capability to merge several copies of a document that have been reviewed and modified by different people. All the comments and revision changes from each copy are merged into one document.

> **NOTE** This feature is not available in Word 6.0 or Word 95.

You can easily identify the revisions because Word underlines and changes the text color of all revisions and highlights comments. Position your mouse pointer next to the underlined or highlighted words, and a pop-up displays the name of the person making the change, the date the change was made, and what type of change was made.

To merge documents you must first open one of the documents (perhaps the original), and then choose Tools, Merge Documents. The Select File to Merge Into Current Document dialog box appears, as shown in Figure 2.34. Identify the file with which you want to merge the current file.

If you need to merge several files into the current file, repeat the Merge Documents command until all files have been merged. If several people have edited the same word or phrase, all edits are shown together so you can decide which one to accept.

FIG. 2.34 ▶

Word 97 merge feature

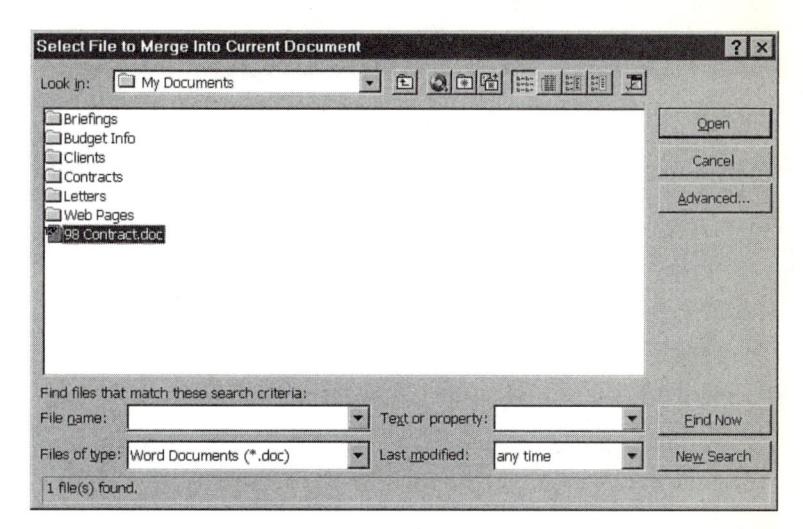

Tracking Revisions
Reviewing Document Changes

When revisions are made to a Word document, in any version, the changes are color coded to indicate who made the changes. An enhancement has been added to Word 97 when you are tracking revisions or edits made by others to documents. You can quickly alternate between three settings:

- View the changes with highlighting (underlines and color)
- View the changes without highlighting
- View the original text, without the changes

This enables you to look at the changes proposed by others, see the changes implemented (deleted text removed), and compare the changes to the original text.

Figure 2.35 shows the Review Revisions dialog box in Word 95. The comparable dialog box in Word 97, the Accept or Reject Changes dialog box, appears in Figure 2.36.

> **NOTE** In both Word 95 and Word 97, these dialog boxes will remain on the screen as you scroll around the document, edit data, change views, and even display other documents.

Upgrading to Microsoft Word 95 and Word 97

FIG. 2.35 ▶
Word 95

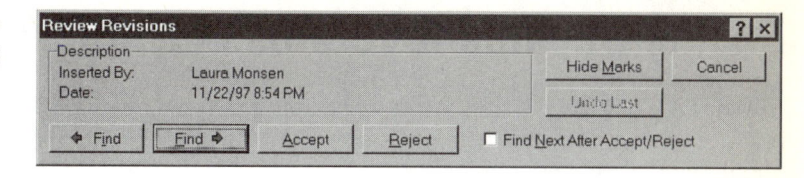

A new feature in Word 97

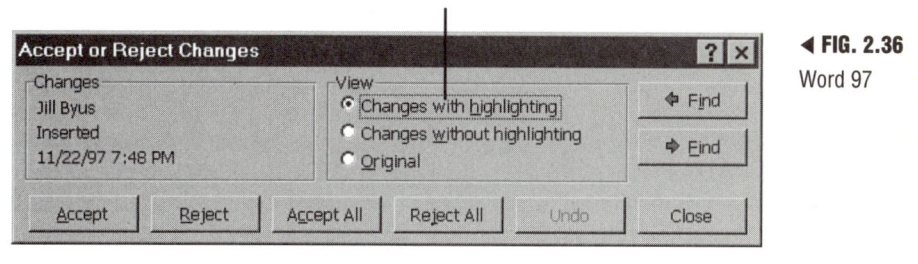

◀ FIG. 2.36
Word 97

Tracking Revisions

Saving Document Versions (Word 97 Only)

In Word 6.0 (Office 4.3) and Word 95, keeping different versions of a document requires you to save each version as a separate file. In Word 97, you can save different versions of a document within the same file. To distinguish one version from another, Word prompts you to add a comment to each version.

To save a version of a document, choose File, Versions. The Versions In dialog box appears, as shown in Figure 2.37. Choose the Save Now button, and the Save Version dialog box appears (see Figure 2.38). Type in any comments that will help distinguish this version from other versions.

To open a version, choose File, Versions and select the version you want to open.

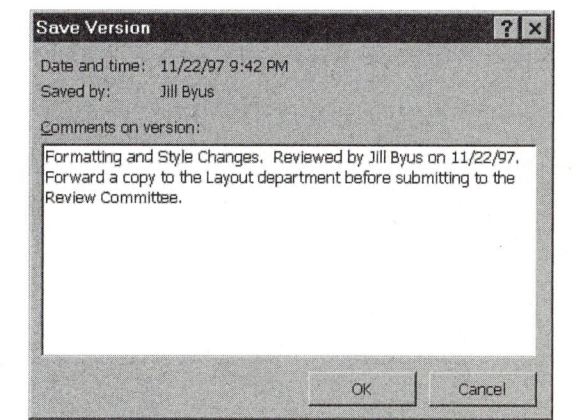

Upgrading to Microsoft Word 95 and Word 97

◀ **FIG. 2.37**
Word 97 Versions In dialog box

Save a version each time you close a file

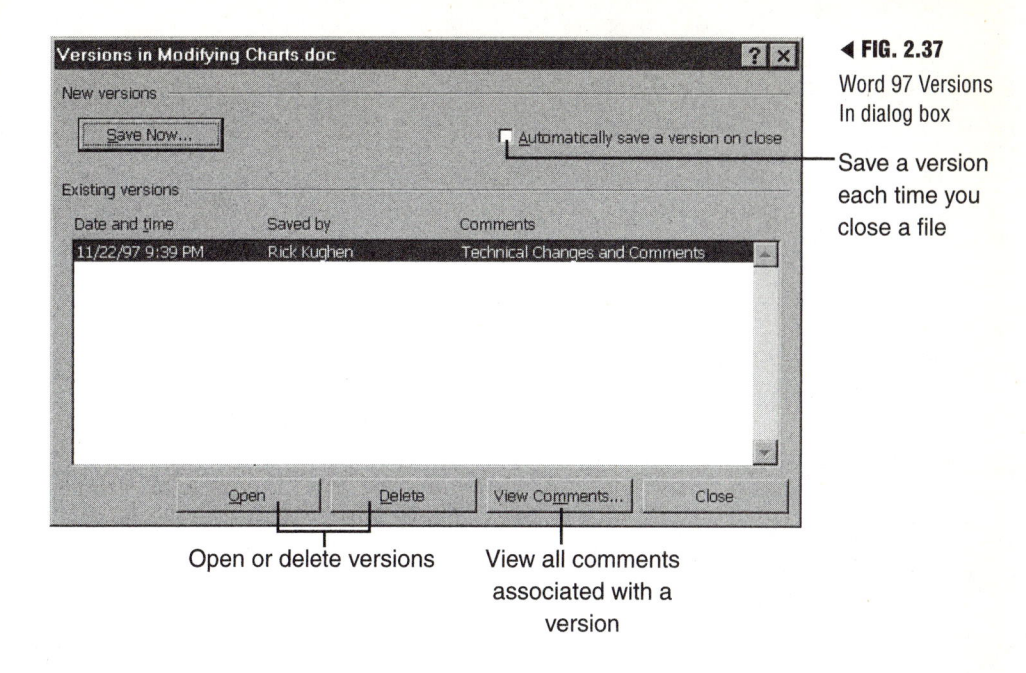

Open or delete versions   View all comments associated with a version

FIG. 2.38 ▶
Word 97 Save Version dialog box

3

Upgrading to Microsoft Excel 95 and Excel 97

IF YOU ARE MIGRATING FROM Office 4.3 to Office 95 or Office 97, you will be pleased with the new and enhanced features that have been added to Excel. Some of the features introduced in this chapter are

- **Managing Files.** Convert files created in previous versions of Excel to your current version of Excel. Save your Excel files in HTML format so they can be used as Web pages.
- **Editing and Formatting.** See how to merge several cells into one cell. Use the AutoComplete feature to expedite data entry. Apply different formats to cells based on the type of data in the cell.
- **Formulas and Functions.** Create functions more easily with the enhanced Paste Function option.
- **Charts and Maps.** Create regional and global maps using data in your worksheets. Explore the enhanced Chart Wizard, which includes new chart types and options.
- **Workgroup Features.** Allow other members of your workgroup to simultaneously access your workbooks to insert comments or make editing changes.
- **Importing and Exporting Data.** Convert Excel lists into Access tables and quickly create input forms or reports based on the worksheet data. Use the Microsoft Query program to import data from databases into an Excel worksheet.

The following list identifies each version of Excel and the Microsoft Office version with which it is associated. Excel 95 and Excel 97 will be used when referring to those versions.

Excel Version Number	**Microsoft Office Version**
Excel 5.0	Office 4.3
Excel 7.0 (often referred to as Excel 95)	Office 95
Excel 8.0 (often referred to as Excel 97)	Office 97

What's New
Excel 95

The following list describes many of the new or enhanced features in Excel 95:

- **Sharing Lists.** Share workbooks with other users and track the changes made to the workbook. You can enter or sort data, or add rows or columns, but you cannot change cell formatting or modify formulas.
- **Converting Excel Data into Access Tables.** Convert Excel lists into Access tables and quickly create input forms or reports based on the data, all from within Excel.
- **Microsoft Excel Viewer.** Similar to the Viewer in PowerPoint, users who do not have Excel can open and view Excel files you send to them.
- **Plotting Maps.** Worksheet data organized geographically can be plotted on a map, with color coding distinguishing the different data.
- **Built-in Templates.** Templates provide predesigned worksheet forms such as a purchase order, invoice, and expense statement. Data entered into a form can be stored in lists or databases. You can create templates that store data in lists or databases by using the new Template Wizard with Data Tracking.

Additional enhancements and minor changes in Excel 95 include the following:

- Move a range of cells from one workbook or worksheet to another by dragging the border of the selected cells.
- Notes added to cells automatically display when you place the mouse pointer on a cell.
- What's This help, represented by a question mark, is available in all dialog boxes and provides more information on the items in a dialog box.
- As you enter text in a list, Excel compares the characters you are typing with other entries in the same column and completes the entry for you.

Excel 97

Excel 97 includes all the enhancements listed for Excel 95, as well as some additional features. The following list describes the most significant of these new features:

- **Chart Wizard.** Creating charts has never been easier than with the improved Chart Wizard in Excel 97. Several new chart types are available, along with added features such as data tables and screen tips identifying each part of a chart.

Upgrading to Microsoft Excel 95 and Excel 97

- **Editing and Data Entry Enhancements.** Excel 97 allows you to undo multiple actions. You can apply conditional formats to cells and validate data as it is entered into a cell.

- **Internet and intranet Features.** You can save your Excel document in an HTML format (used for Web pages). Create a *hyperlink*, a pointer, from one document to another including Internet Web pages. Access useful information online from Microsoft through the Help menu.

- **Retrieve Data from External Databases.** Use Microsoft Query and the new Query Wizard to set up a data source, connect to a database, select data to retrieve, and even sort or filter the data before bringing it into Excel.

- **Sharing Workbooks.** One person can edit one worksheet in a workbook while someone else can edit another worksheet simultaneously. When one user saves the workbook, the other users who share it see the changes made by that user. Different people can access adjacent data in the same worksheet. The shared workbook feature replaces the shared list feature in Microsoft Excel 95.

- **Workgroup Features.** You can merge copies of a workbook to consolidate comments and editing changes. A new toolbar, the Comments and Review toolbar, enables you to quickly view all comments made to a shared workbook. The Microsoft Binder lets you group documents from different programs into a single place for editing and review.

- **Worksheet Function Changes.** The Paste Function command replaces the Function Wizard. You can collapse (and expand) a dialog box to select cell ranges in your worksheets while using a function. Additional worksheet functions have been added to Excel.

Following are some additional enhancements and minor changes in Excel 97:

- The maximum number of worksheet rows has increased from 16,384 to 65,536.

- The default number of worksheets in a new workbook has been reduced from 16 to 3, to avoid storing a large number of empty worksheets.

- Several cells can be merged into one cell. Text in a cell can be indented to provide an informal outline appearance. Data can be angled in a cell or displayed vertically.

Managing Files

Exchanging Files Created in Different Versions of Excel

You can display a file created in an earlier version of Excel simply by opening the file in your current version of Excel. For example, if you have a file that was created in Excel 5.0 and you are currently using Excel 97, open the Excel 5.0 file in Excel 97 to display it.

To convert a file from an earlier version of Excel to a newer version, you must save the file. The following list shows how to save older files into your newer version of Excel:

- **Excel 95.** When you save the file, it is immediately converted into an Excel 95 format.
- **Excel 97.** When you attempt to save a file that was created in an earlier version of Excel, the dialog box displayed in Figure 3.1 appears. You have the choice of saving the file as an Excel 97 file or keeping it as an Excel 5.0 or 95 file.

When you create a file in Excel 95, you do not have to save the file in an Excel 5.0 format in order to open the file in Excel 5.0. Any features unique to Excel 95, such as long filenames, will not be displayed in Excel 5.0. This includes any cell formats that are available only in Excel 95. Figure 3.2 shows the Open dialog box in Excel 5.0. The budget file for 1998 was originally created in Excel 95 and saved as **98 Budget.xls**. Because Windows 3.1 does not allow spaces in filenames and limits the name length to eight characters, **1** the name for this file is converted to **98budg~1.xls**.

When you create a file in Excel 97, you must save the file in an **2** Excel 5.0/95 Workbook or **3** Excel 97 and Excel 5.0/95 Workbook format. This will allow you to open the file in these versions of Excel. Figure 3.3 shows an example of the Save As dialog box in Excel 97 and the choices you have for changing the file type.

> **TIP** Type **converting files** in the Office Assistant (Excel 97) search box for a list of several help screens, including one entitled *Formatting and features not transferred in file conversions*.

Upgrading to Microsoft Excel 95 and Excel 97

FIG. 3.1 ▶
Excel 97 update dialog box

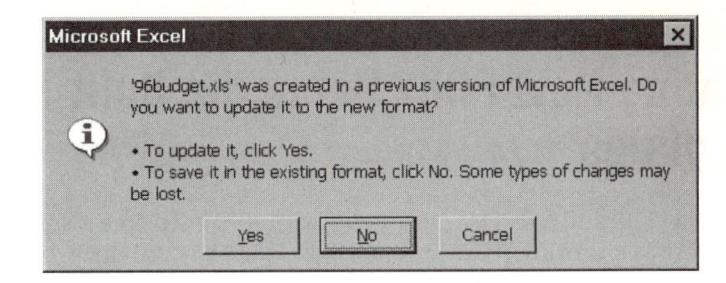

FIG. 3.2 ▶
Excel 5.0 Open dialog box

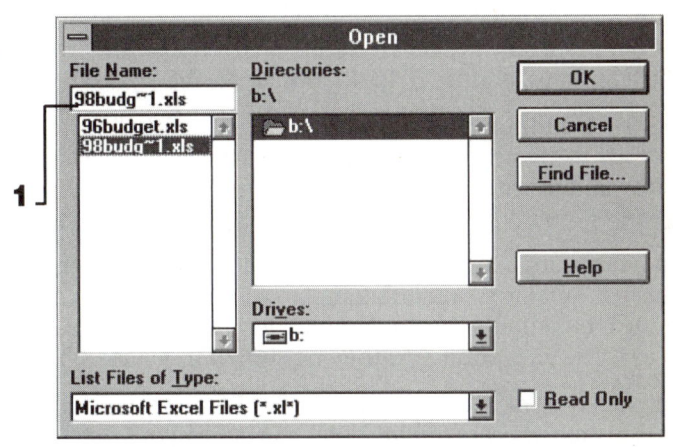

FIG. 3.3 ▶
Excel 97 Save As dialog box

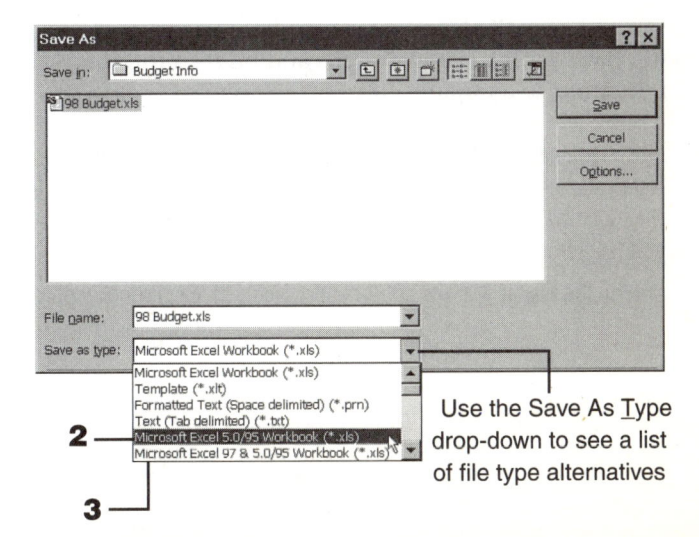

Use the Save As Type drop-down to see a list of file type alternatives

61

Managing Files

Creating New Files Using the Built-in Templates

New in Excel 95 and Excel 97 are a series of predesigned spreadsheet files, which you can use as a starting point for new files. Excel 95 contained 10 templates, whereas Excel 97 contains only three templates. Initially, it may seem odd that there are fewer templates in Excel 97. The three templates in Excel 97 are the most popular templates from Excel 95, and were enhanced and updated for Excel 97. Additionally, new templates and many of the templates from Excel 95 can be downloaded from Microsoft's Excel Free Stuff Web page on the Internet. To download these free templates, choose Help, Microsoft on the Web, Free Stuff.

If you use the New button on the Standard toolbar, the Workbook template is automatically used to create the file. You must use the File, New command to see a list of the built-in templates.

When you choose the File, New command in Excel 95 or Excel 97, a dialog box with several tabs appears. The default Workbook template is on the **1** General tab, which contains the default Workbook template. The Spreadsheet Solutions tab, shown in Figure 3.4, contains the predesigned templates. The Spreadsheet Solutions tab in Excel 95 is similar to the one shown in Figure 3.4.

If you have upgraded from Excel 95, the **2** Office 95 templates will be listed on their own tab. This tab appears only if Excel 95 was on your machine when Excel 97 was installed. A **3** preview of the selected template appears on the right side of the dialog box.

When you create a new file based on a template, a copy of the template opens. The templates have sophisticated designs and built-in formulas. Figure 3.5 shows a sample of the Invoice template.

> **NOTE** Some templates contain macros. You may see a warning message that indicates the template contains macros and the computer viruses are usually hidden in macros. This is a very good warning when you open files, especially if those files came from other users or off the Internet.
>
> Choose the Enable Macros button to proceed with displaying a copy of the template.

Upgrading to Microsoft Excel 95 and Excel 97

◄ **FIG. 3.4**
Excel 97 Spreadsheet Solutions tab

FIG. 3.5 ►
Excel 97 Invoice template

Provides help and formatting options

Note indicator

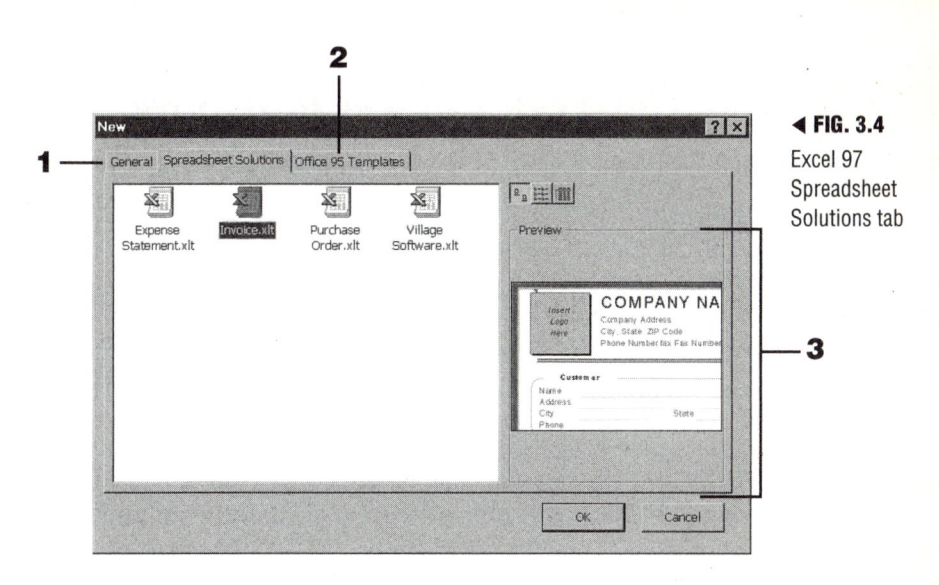

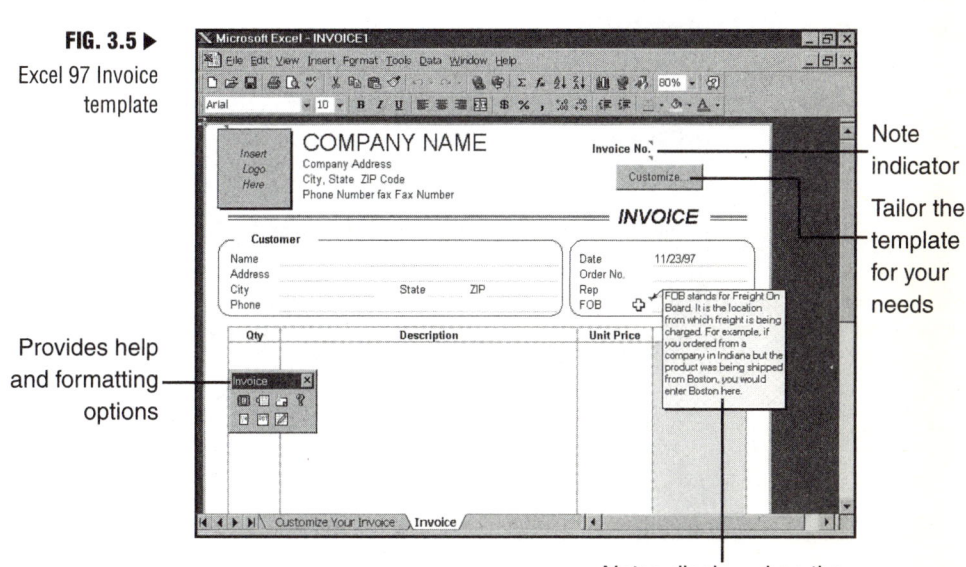

Tailor the template for your needs

Notes display when the mouse pointer is close to the note indicator

63

Managing Files

Saving Files in HTML Format (Excel 97 Only)

New in Excel 97 is the capability to save data and charts from Excel worksheets into a format that can be used for Web pages on the Internet or your company's internal intranet. This format is known as *Hypertext Markup Language* or *HTML*. A wizard will assist you in converting your Excel data into an HTML file.

To access this wizard, choose File, Save as HTML. The Internet Assistant Wizard displays the first step in the conversion process, as shown in Figure 3.6. In this step, choose which cells or charts in the Excel worksheet you want to convert. In step 2, shown in Figure 3.7, you can have the data converted into a new file or inserted into an existing HTML file. Figure 3.8 shows step 3 in the Internet Assistant Wizard. In this step, you type information, such as Title, Header, dividing lines, and an email address, that you want to appear in the converted file. Step 4, shown in Figure 3.9, is where you select the location in which you want the converted file to be stored.

FIG. 3.6 ▶
Step 1

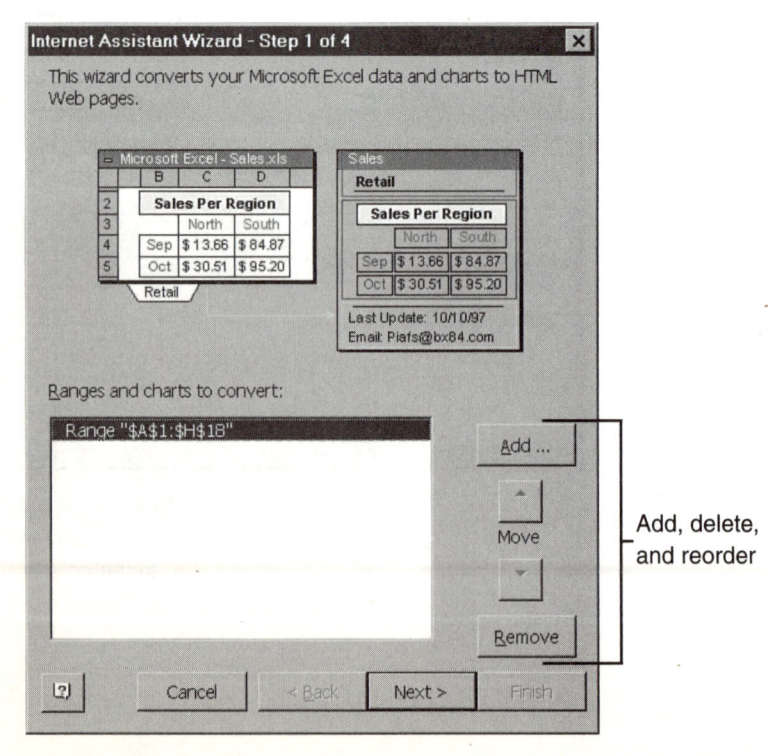

Upgrading to Microsoft Excel 95 and Excel 97

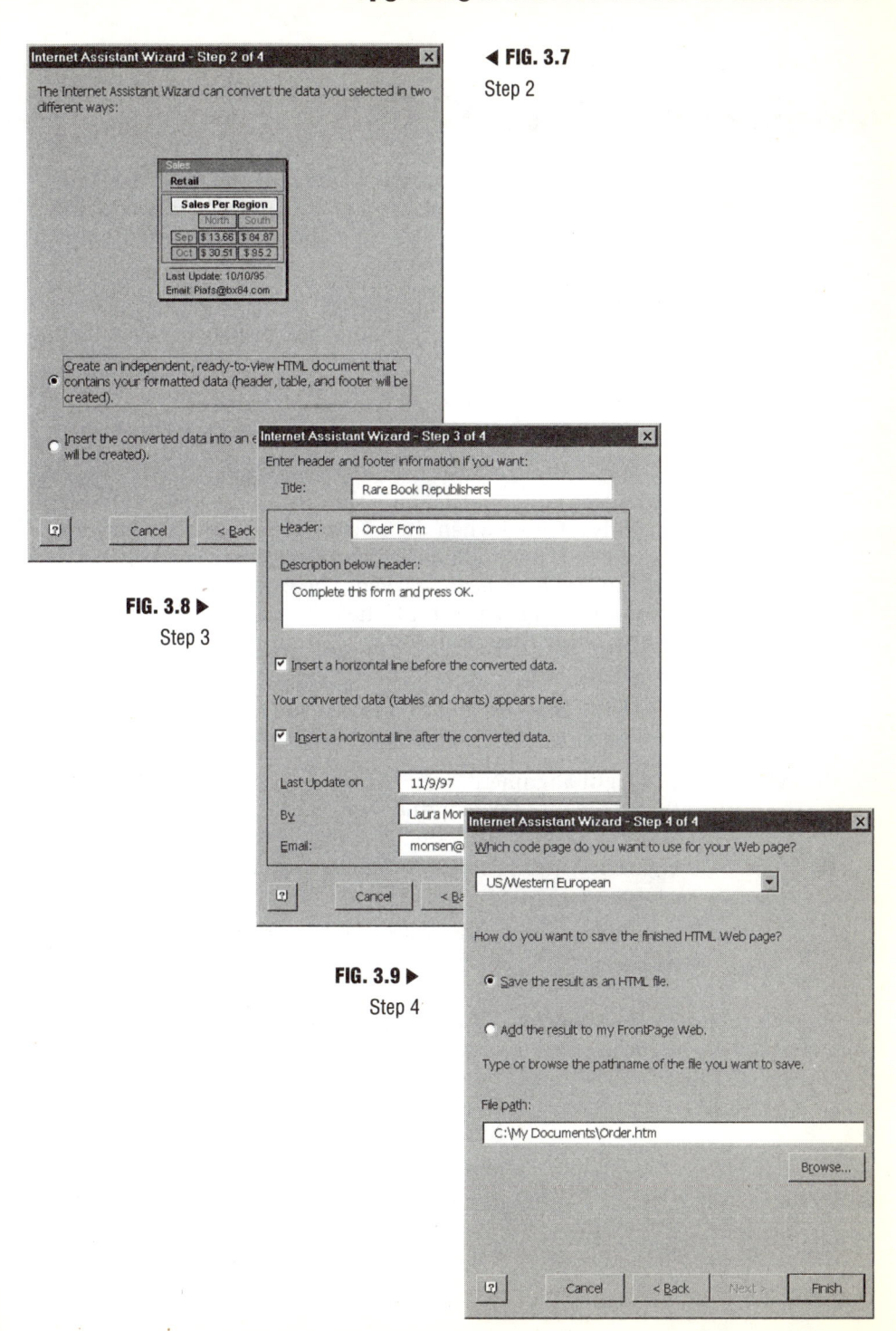

◀ FIG. 3.7
Step 2

FIG. 3.8 ▶
Step 3

FIG. 3.9 ▶
Step 4

Editing and Formatting
Merging Cells (Excel 97 Only)

A new feature added to Excel 97 is the capability to merge several cells into one cell. Though merging cells may appear similar to a feature in Excel for centering data across several columns, merging is, in fact, quite different. Figure 3.10 illustrates both **1** merged cells and **2** centered data.

Merging physically combines several cells into one cell in the worksheet. Centering data across several columns simply changes the display of the data; the cells remain unchanged.

When cells are merged, the upper-leftmost cell reference becomes the reference for the merged cells. In the first example of merged cells in Figure 3.10, the cell reference for the merged cells is B2 (C2, D2, and E2 no longer exist).

If the cells you select to merge contain data, only the data in the upper-left cell of the selected group of cells is retained when the cells are merged. Excel will warn you that all other data will be lost if you proceed to merge the cells. In Figure 3.10, **3** the cells B7 through D8 have been selected. The **4** warning message appears when you attempt to merge the cells. If the cells are merged in this example, only **1997** is retained, while **Budget** is lost.

The Center Across Columns button, available on the Formatting toolbar in Excel 5.0 and Excel 95, has become **5** Merge and Center in Excel 97. When you use this button, the selected cells are merged, and the data is centered in the merged cells.

Use the Left, Center, or Right alignment buttons on the Formatting toolbar to change the horizontal alignment of data in the merged cells.

> **NOTE** The **6** Merge Cells option is also available on the Alignment tab in the Format Cells dialog box (see Figure 3.11).
>
> Use the **7** Horizontal alignment options in the Format Cells dialog box to center data across several columns.

To split cells that have been merged, clear the Merge Cells check box on the Alignment tab of the Format Cells dialog box (see Figure 3.11).

Upgrading to Microsoft Excel 95 and Excel 97

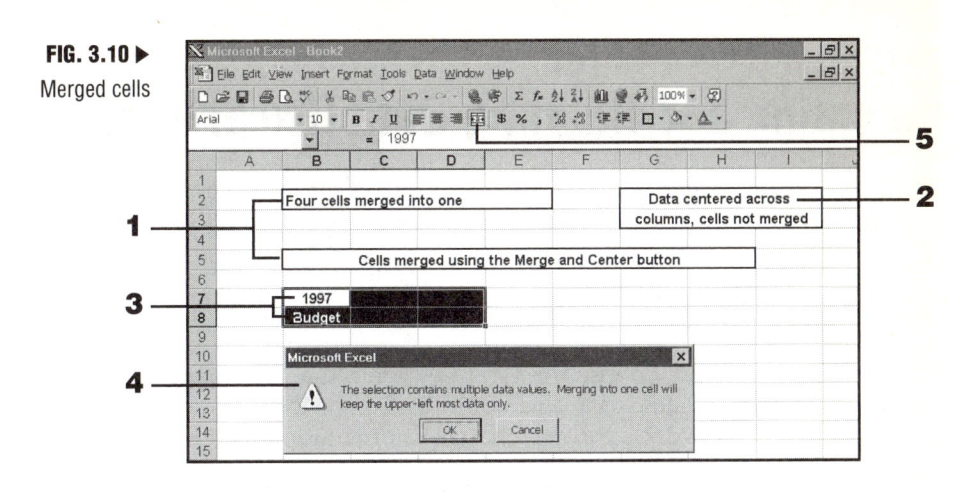

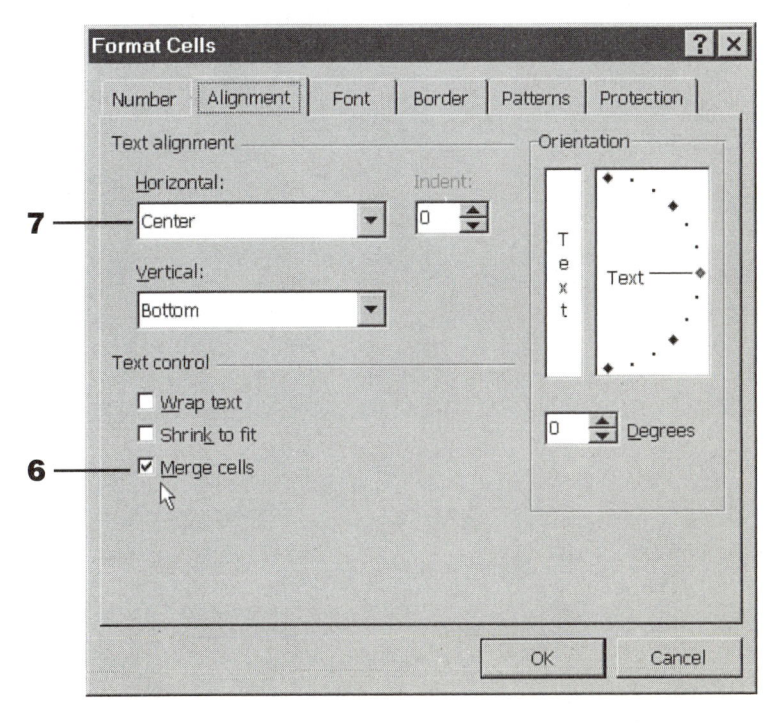

FIG. 3.10 ▶
Merged cells

◀ FIG. 3.11
Format Cells dialog box

Editing and Formatting

Indenting and Rotating Data (Excel 97 Only)

To enhance the appearance of the data in your worksheets, Excel 97 includes two new formatting options: indenting and rotating.

Data can be indented inside a cell, up to 15 levels. You can rotate data in a cell from 90 degrees to –90 degrees, at 1-degree increments, or display the data vertically.

To indent or rotate data, choose Format, Cells. From the Alignment tab (see Figure 3.12), select the desired **1** levels of indention or **2** degrees of rotation. Instead of rotating the data, you can change its orientation data to **3** vertical.

You can also indent data with the **4** Decrease Indent and **5** Increase Indent buttons on the Formatting toolbar, shown in Figure 3.13.

Figure 3.13 shows an example of using **6** rotating and **7** indenting data to enhance a worksheet.

Upgrading to Microsoft Excel 95 and Excel 97

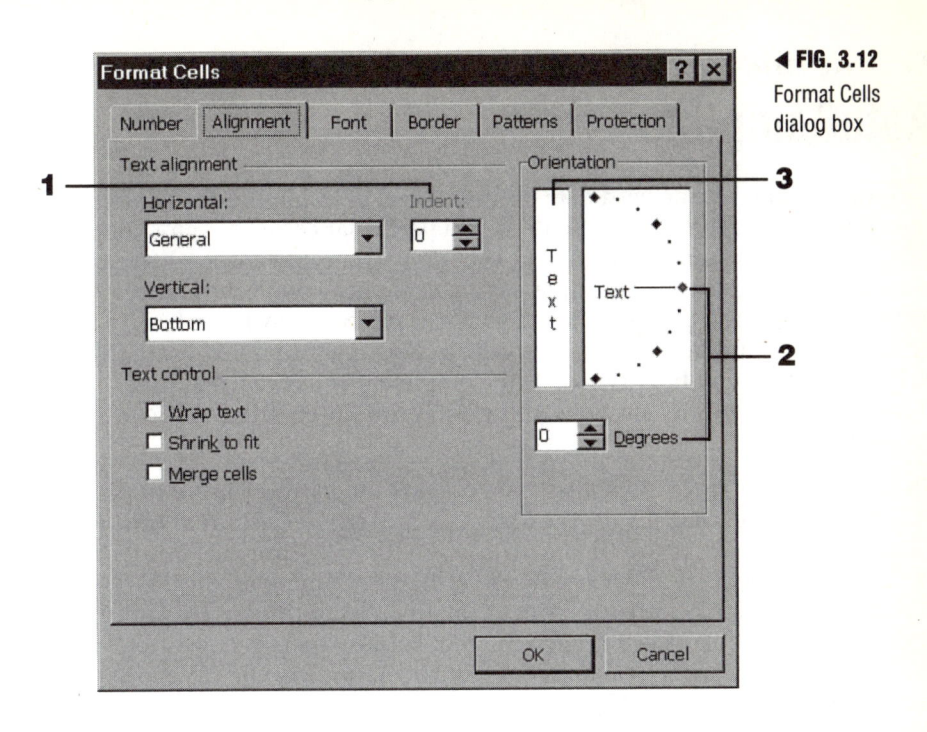

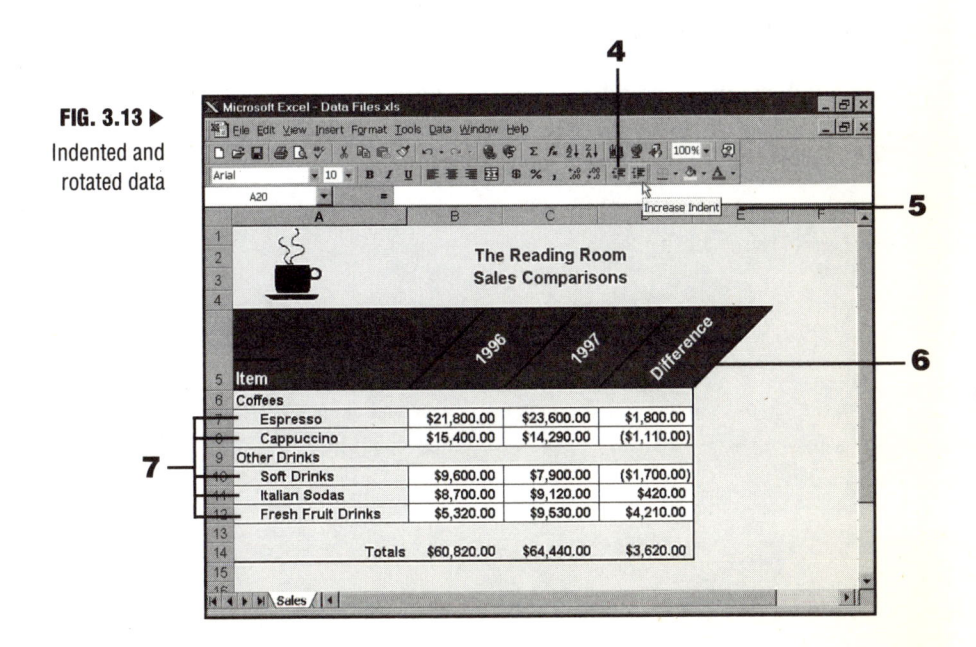

◄ **FIG. 3.12**
Format Cells dialog box

FIG. 3.13 ►
Indented and rotated data

Editing and Formatting
AutoComplete

You will spend less time with data entry in Excel by using the AutoComplete feature. If you have repetitive text entries in a particular column, AutoComplete can help you enter the text more quickly, especially when the entries differ after the second or third letter. AutoComplete is available in Excel 95 and Excel 97. AutoComplete compares the characters you type in a cell with entries in the same column, above and below the active cell. If there is another text entry that matches the characters you have typed, AutoComplete fills in the remaining characters. If AutoComplete fills in the entry you want, press Enter; otherwise, continue to type your entry.

The example in Figure 3.14 shows a list of book orders and a list of music orders. Several of the cities begin with the letters *Ca*: **Calgary**, **Calcutta**, **Canberra**, **Cairo**, and **Cannes**. If you type **Can** in cell A10, AutoComplete fills in the remaining letters of the city **Canberra**. Although Cannes also begins with *Can* in column A, Excel looks only for entries that are in a continuous list and stops at the point where a blank cell is encountered. Because there is at least one blank line between the list of city names in Figure 3.14, none of the city names in the second list will be proposed by AutoComplete when entering names in the first list.

AutoComplete duplicates the capitalization used in the first occurrence of the word. In this example, if you type **ca**, where the letter *c* is not capitalized, Canberra will be capitalized when you press Enter.

NOTE AutoComplete does not work with numbers.

Upgrading to Microsoft Excel 95 and Excel 97

FIG. 3.14 ▶
Excel 95 and 97 AutoComplete

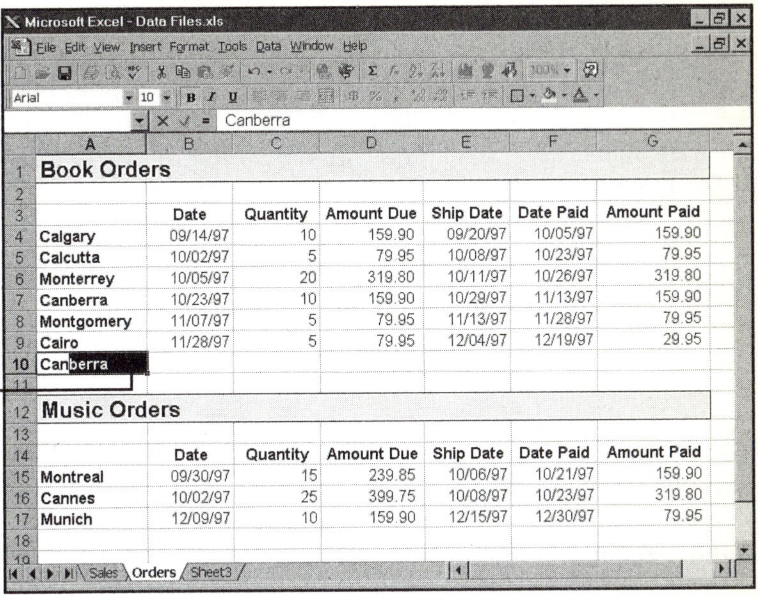

AutoComplete proposes the remaining text

	A	B	C	D	E	F	G
1	**Book Orders**						
2							
3		Date	Quantity	Amount Due	Ship Date	Date Paid	Amount Paid
4	Calgary	09/14/97	10	159.90	09/20/97	10/05/97	159.90
5	Calcutta	10/02/97	5	79.95	10/08/97	10/23/97	79.95
6	Monterrey	10/05/97	20	319.80	10/11/97	10/26/97	319.80
7	Canberra	10/23/97	10	159.90	10/29/97	11/13/97	159.90
8	Montgomery	11/07/97	5	79.95	11/13/97	11/28/97	79.95
9	Cairo	11/28/97	5	79.95	12/04/97	12/19/97	29.95
10	Can**berra**						
11							
12	**Music Orders**						
13							
14		Date	Quantity	Amount Due	Ship Date	Date Paid	Amount Paid
15	Montreal	09/30/97	15	239.85	10/06/97	10/21/97	159.90
16	Cannes	10/02/97	25	399.75	10/08/97	10/23/97	319.80
17	Munich	12/09/97	10	159.90	12/15/97	12/30/97	79.95

71

Editing and Formatting

Validating Data Entry (Excel 97 Only)

The Data Validation command is a new, powerful feature in Excel 97. Through this command, you have three options for controlling data entry:

- You can control the data that can be entered in a cell by displaying a list of choices or by placing restrictions (limits) on the entries.
- You can create input messages that instruct users on the appropriate data to be entered in a cell.
- You can display an error message if incorrect data is entered in a cell or have Excel draw circles around invalid entries in the worksheet.

You can use these three options separately or in conjunction with one another.

To validate the data that is entered in a cell, choose Data, Validation. The Settings tab, shown in Figure 3.15, is where you select the type of data you want to allow in the cell. The **1** validation criteria options displayed on the Settings tab change based on your selection.

The **2** Input Message tab of the Data Validation dialog box is used to create a message that instructs users on the type of data expected in the cell. The **3** Error Alert tab of the Data Validation dialog box is used to create a message that displays when an invalid entry is made. Choose the Circle Invalid Data button on the Auditing toolbar to draw circles around cells in the worksheet.

FIG. 3.15 ▶

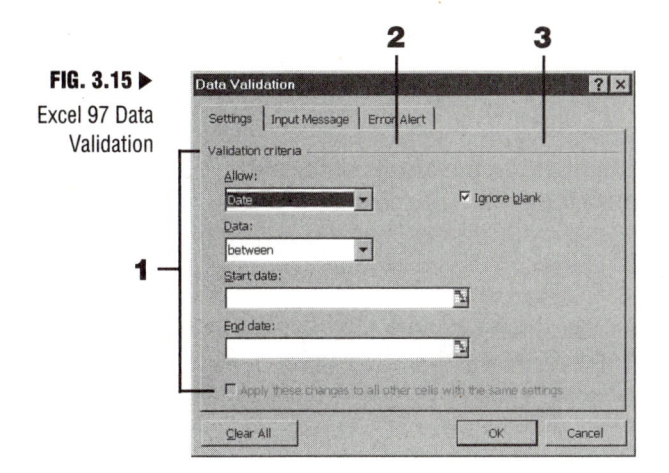

Excel 97 Data Validation

Editing and Formatting

Applying Conditional Formats (Excel 97 Only)

A powerful new number-formatting feature has been added to Excel 97 that makes it easy to format a cell based on the data in the cell. Conditional formatting is especially useful for highlighting the results of formulas. You can specify up to three conditional formats for a cell.

Figure 3.16 shows the appearance of a worksheet before and after conditional formatting. In this example:

- If the % Change is negative, the cell displays light gray shading. The % Change for **1** Colorado has gray shading.
- If the % Change is between 5% and 15%, the cell displays in bold font. The % Change for **2** Virginia is in bold.
- If the % Change is 15% or higher, the cell displays in bold and italic. The % Change for **3** Wyoming is displayed in bold and italic.

There is no specific condition if the % Change is between 0% and 5% (therefore, the cells for California and Texas); the formatting that already exists in the cell remains.

The Conditional Formatting dialog box, shown in Figure 3.17, lists the formats applied to the % Change cells in Figure 3.16. Choose F_o_rmat, Con_d_itional Formatting to access this dialog box.

> **NOTE** If conditional formatting is added to a cell that has a formula, when the formula is copied, the conditional formatting is copied, too.

Upgrading to Microsoft Excel 95 and Excel 97

◀ **FIG. 3.16**

Excel 97 Conditional formatting

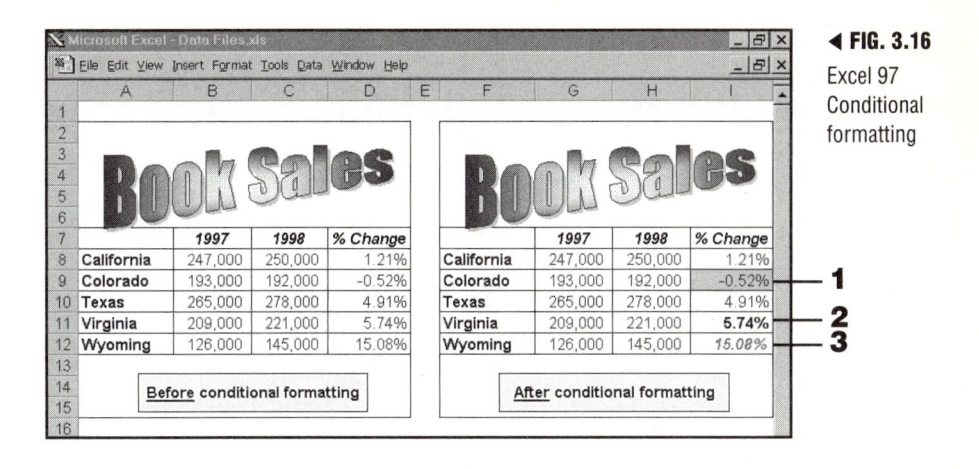

FIG. 3.17 ▶

Conditional Formatting dialog box

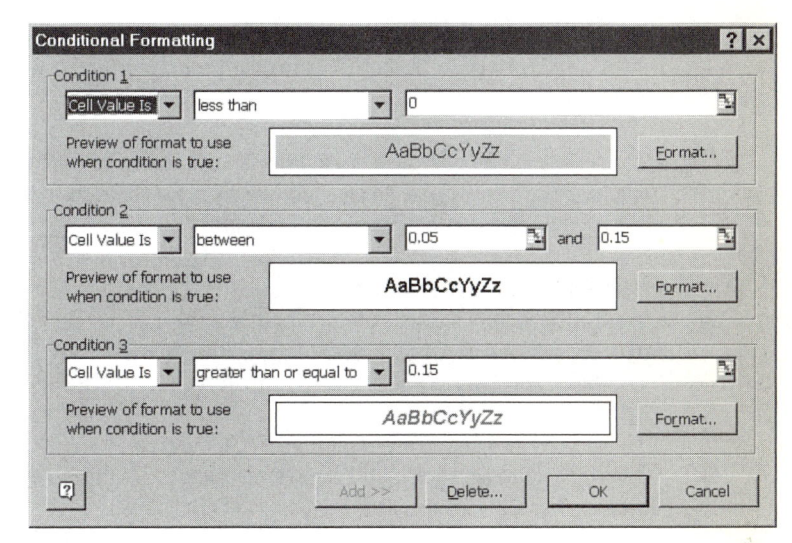

75

Editing and Formatting
Displaying and Reviewing Embedded Comments

Attaching notes to cells is a feature that has been available since Excel 5.0. In both Excel 95 and Excel 97, this feature was enhanced; in Excel 97, it was renamed *Comments*. Attaching comments to cells is especially useful in forms or templates inside of which other people will be inputting data. Comments are a means of preventing errors and providing explanations in worksheets.

Figure 3.18 shows a worksheet with built-in comments. Comments can be attached to any cell. Excel places **1** an indicator in the upper-right corner of each cell that contains a comment. The indicator is a red triangle. New in Excel 95, when you position the mouse pointer in the cell, the comment automatically appears on the screen. In Excel 97, **2** the author of the comment is included with the comment, and **3** a new toolbar, the Reviewing toolbar, has been designed especially for creating and reading comments.

To create or edit a comment in Excel 95, choose Insert, Note. In Excel 97, choose Insert, Comment.

> **TIP** The bold title in the comment is taken from the User Name box on the General tab of the Options dialog box. You can edit the text directly in the comment in the worksheet, making each title unique to that particular comment.

To print worksheet comments, choose File, Page Setup, and select the Sheet tab in the Page Setup dialog box. Comments are printed on a separate page. In Excel 97 you can print the comments in the worksheet. You must first display the comments on the worksheet by choosing the Comment and Indicator setting on the View tab of the Options dialog box.

> **NOTE** The Page Setup dialog box must be accessed from the File menu, not through the Print Preview screen, to choose one of the Comment print options.

Upgrading to Microsoft Excel 95 and Excel 97

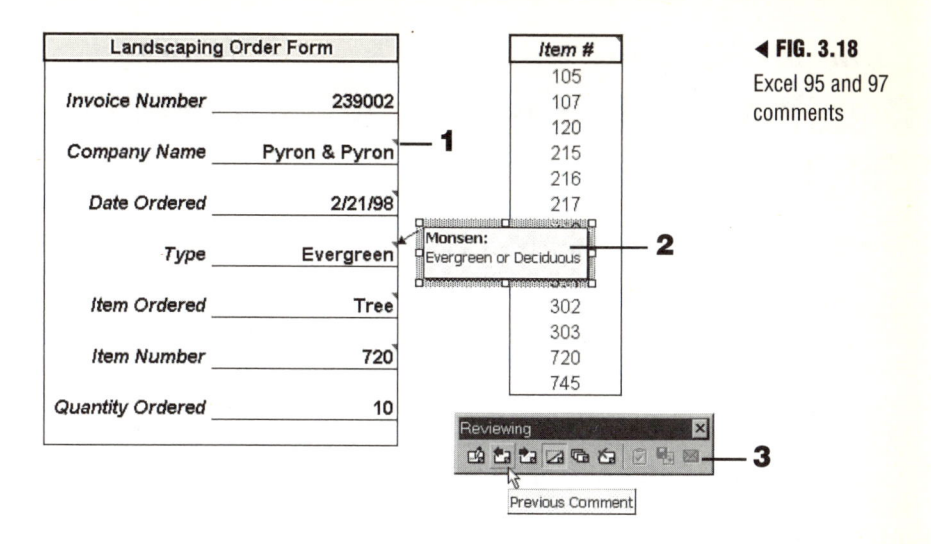

◄ **FIG. 3.18**

Excel 95 and 97 comments

Formulas and Functions

Creating and Editing Formulas (Excel 97 Only)

Several new enhancements have been added to Excel 97 that make it easier to create and edit formulas, especially if you use worksheet functions. In Excel 5.0 and Excel 95, when you want to use a function, you either type in the function or select the Function Wizard button on the Standard toolbar. In Excel 97, **1** Paste Function replaces the Function Wizard. The Paste Function command expands on the features that were part of the Function Wizard, making it easier to use the built-in worksheet functions.

Figure 3.19 shows the **2** Paste Function dialog box. The **3** Office Assistant appears, asking if you need help using the dialog box. If you don't know which function to use, select Yes in the Office Assistant pop-up and type a description of what you want to do. The Office Assistant will suggest which worksheet functions to use.

Once you select the function to use, choose OK. A dialog box for the function you selected appears (see Figure 3.20). This dialog box is referred to as the Formula Palette. The Paste Function dialog box is anchored below the **4** Formula Bar. This dialog box displays **5** a description of the function and each argument.

Often, Excel selects the range of cells to use in the function. In this example, Excel has **6** selected cells B4:B15. This would create an inaccurate average, because the Year Total in cell B15 is included in the range. A new feature in this dialog box enables you to **7** collapse the dialog box to more easily select cells in your worksheet. Once you have selected the cells, you can then expand the dialog box by using the same button.

> **TIP** You cannot select range names from the Name box on the Formula Bar while the Formula Palette is displayed. To include range names in a formula, press F3.

Upgrading to Microsoft Excel 95 and Excel 97

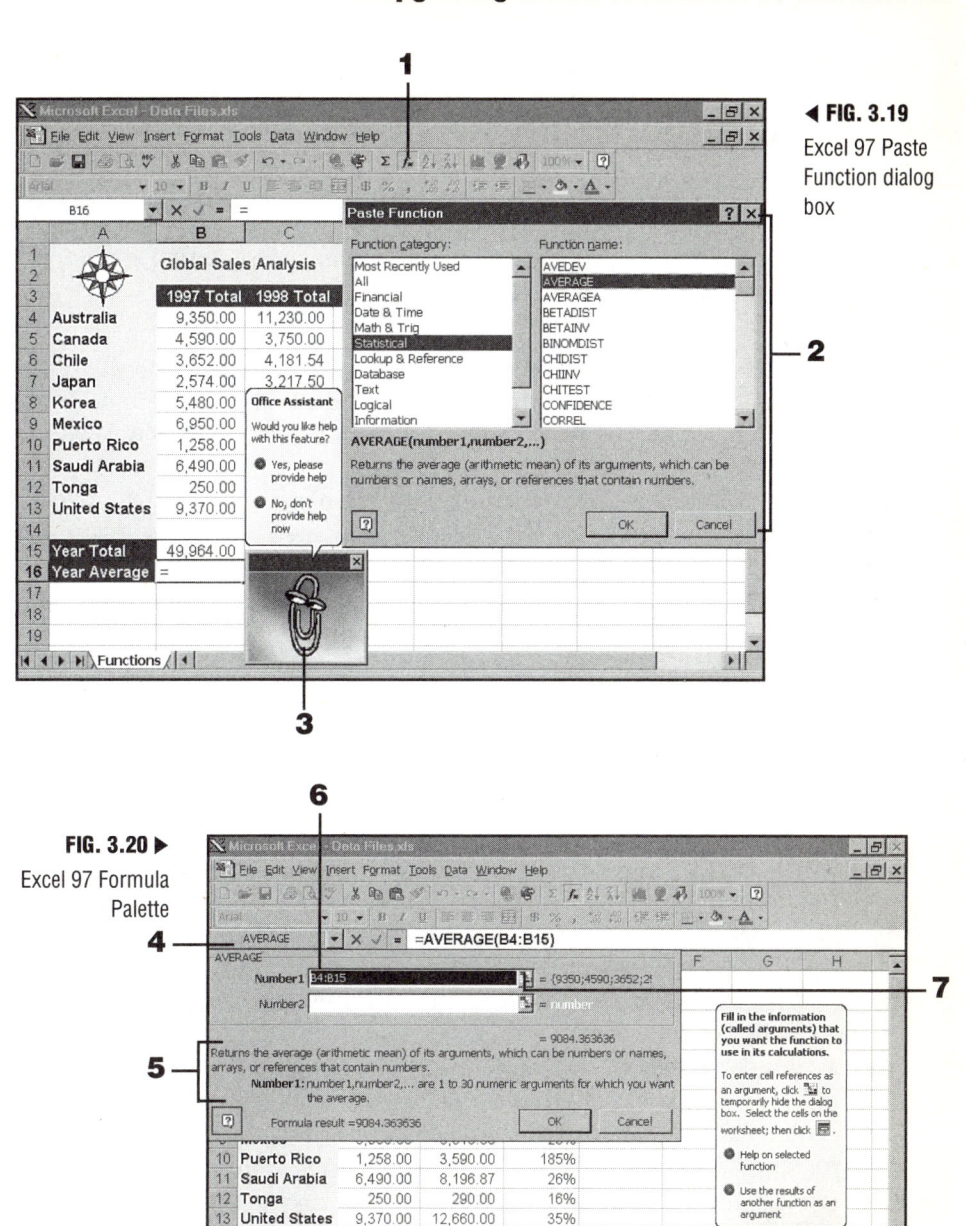

◀ **FIG. 3.19**
Excel 97 Paste Function dialog box

FIG. 3.20 ▶
Excel 97 Formula Palette

79

Formulas and Functions
New Functions (Excel 97 Only)

Several new functions have been added in Excel 97. All functions available to older versions of Excel are available to Excel 97. Figure 3.21 compares the AVERAGE function to the AVERAGEA function. The **1** formula for the AVERAGEA function appears in the Formula Bar. The following table lists new functions found in Excel 97:

- **AVERAGEA.** Similar to AVERAGE. Returns the average of the values in a range of cells. In addition to numbers, cells that contain text and logical values such as TRUE and FALSE are included in the calculation, which AVERAGE does not do.
- **GETPIVOTDATA.** Retrieves data from a PivotTable.
- **HYPERLINK.** Creates a shortcut or jump that opens a document stored on a network server, an intranet, or the Internet.
- **MAXA.** Similar to MAX. Returns the largest value in a range of cells. In addition to numbers, cells that contain text and logical values such as TRUE and FALSE are included in the calculation, which MAX does not do.
- **MINA.** Similar to MIN. Returns the minimum value in a range of cells. In addition to numbers, cells that contain text and logical values such as TRUE and FALSE are included in the calculation, which MIN does not do.
- **STDEVA.** Similar to STDEV. Estimates standard deviation based on a sample of a population. In addition to numbers, cells that contain text and logical values such as TRUE and FALSE are included in the calculation, which STDEV does not do.
- **STDEVPA.** Similar to STDEVP. Calculates standard deviation based on an entire population. In addition to numbers, cells that contain text and logical values such as TRUE and FALSE are included in the calculation, which STDEVP does not do.
- **VARA.** Similar to VAR. Estimates the variance of a sample of a population. In addition to numbers, cells that contain text and logical values such as TRUE and FALSE are included in the calculation, which VAR does not do.
- **VARPA.** Similar to VARP. Calculates the variance based on the entire population. In addition to numbers, cells that contain text and logical values such as TRUE and FALSE are included in the calculation, which VARP does not do.

Upgrading to Microsoft Excel 95 and Excel 97

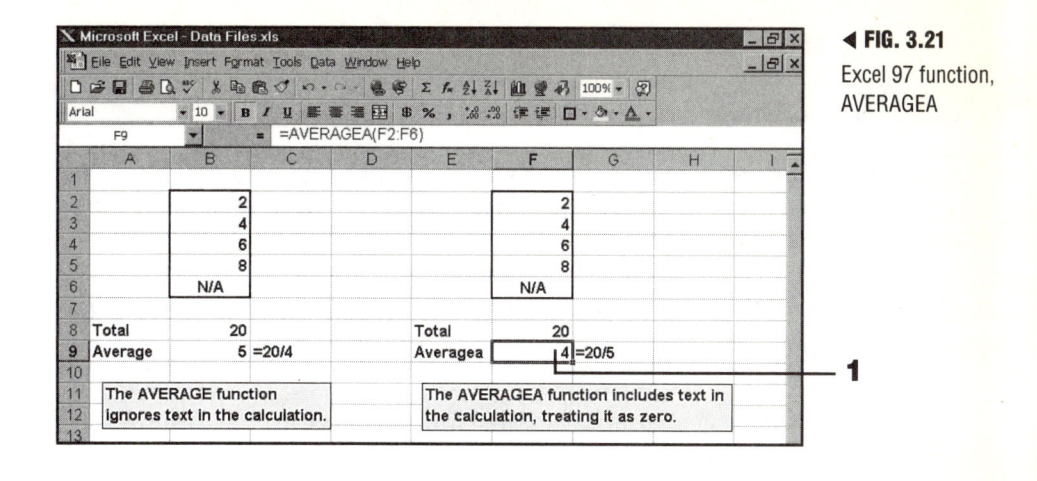

◄ **FIG. 3.21**

Excel 97 function, AVERAGEA

Analyzing Worksheets
Filtering Lists

The AutoFilter feature was introduced in Excel 5.0 (Office 4.3), making it easier to display a *subset* of a list of information in Excel. AutoFilter displays multiple rows (records) matching criteria you specify. You can filter based on an item in the list or create a custom filter in which you can include AND and OR conditions.

In Excel 95, a new option—Top 10—was added to AutoFilter. This feature displays the ten most common values in the selected column. The Top 10 filter is identical in Excel 95 and Excel 97.

Figure 3.22 shows an Excel 97 list of employee information with the **1** AutoFilter active. A filter showing the employees who earn the **Top 15 Percent** of all salaries has been applied to the list. The **2** Top 10 AutoFilter dialog box shows the criteria selected for this filter. Although the name implies you can display the top ten, you actually have much more flexibility than that:

- **3 Portion of the list.** Choose to display the Top or Bottom portion of the list.
- **4 Amount.** Choose any number between 1 and 500.
- **5 Type of information.** Choose to display the amount of items or the amount as a percentage of the whole list.

Figure 3.23 shows the same list of employees, this time with the **Top 15 Items** as the criteria for the filter.

> **NOTE** The Top 10 AutoFilter can be used only on columns that contain numbers or dates. It cannot be applied to columns that contain text.

Upgrading to Microsoft Excel 95 and Excel 97

FIG. 3.22 ▶
Excel 97—Top 10 AutoFilter displaying a percent

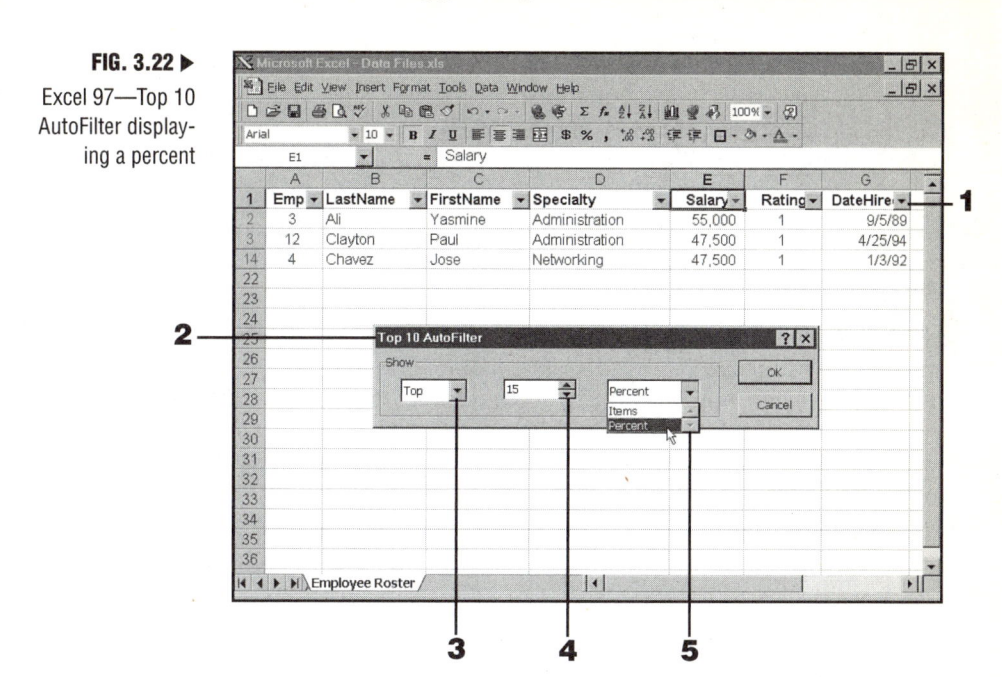

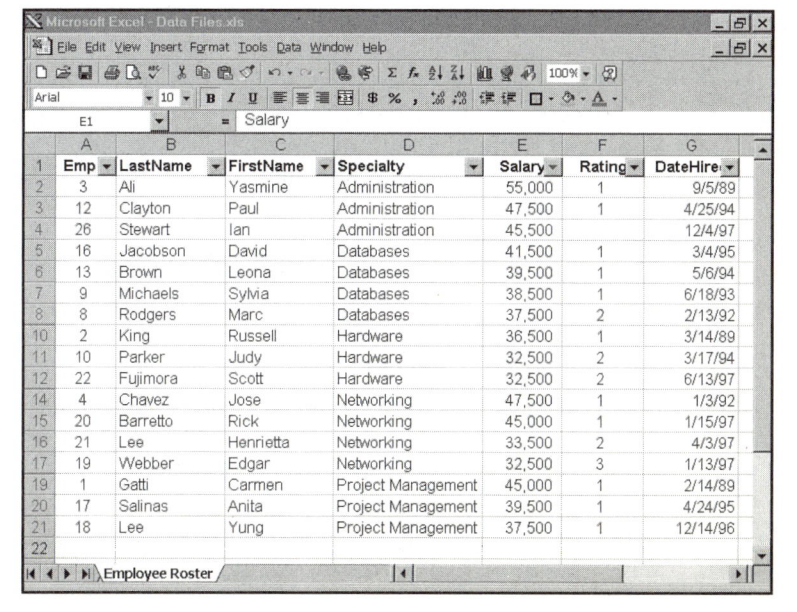

◀ FIG. 3.23
Excel 97—Top 10 AutoFilter displaying a number of items

83

Analyzing Worksheets
Pivot Table Improvements

Pivot tables, a new feature in Excel 5.0, replaces the crosstab tables feature in earlier versions of Excel. The PivotTable Wizard was included in Excel 5.0 to assist users in selecting data for the pivot table and continues to be a valuable tool in Excel 95 and Excel 97.

Many pivot table enhancements have been added in Excel 97. Options that affect the entire pivot table are controlled in a separate PivotTable Options dialog box, as shown in Figure 3.24. You can access this dialog box from the final step (step 4 of 4) in the PivotTable Wizard or from the **1** PivotTable button on the PivotTable toolbar (see Figure 3.25). Some of the enhancements made to Excel pivot tables include the following:

- **Selecting part of a pivot table.** You can select parts of the pivot table structure to format or use in formulas using the **2** Select command.
- **Calculated fields and items.** Creating calculated fields and items is located under the **3** Formulas command on the PivotTable toolbar.
- **Automatic sorting.** Items in a pivot table can be sorted automatically, even when the pivot table layout is changed. **4** Choose PivotTable, Field on the PivotTable toolbar and click the Advanced button to locate the sorting options.
- **Page field retrieval options.** When the pivot table is extracting data from a large external database, you can extract each item in a page field as you display that item. **4** Choose PivotTable, Field on the PivotTable toolbar and click the Advanced button to locate the retrieval options.
- **Formatting.** When you apply formatting and AutoFormats to selected parts of a pivot table, the formatting remains even when you refresh the data or change the pivot table layout by using Preserve Formatting under the **5** Options command on the PivotTable toolbar.
- **Errors values or empty cells.** When a pivot table generates an error value or an empty cell, you can program Excel to display something else in the pivot table. The Error value and empty cell options are located under the **5** Options command on the PivotTable toolbar.
- **Running background queries.** You can run a query on an external database in the background so that you can continue working in Microsoft Excel while the data is being retrieved for a pivot table. The Background Queries option is located under the **5** Options command.
- **Using pivot table data in formulas.** The new GETPIVOTDATA worksheet function lets you create formulas that perform calculations using data in pivot tables.

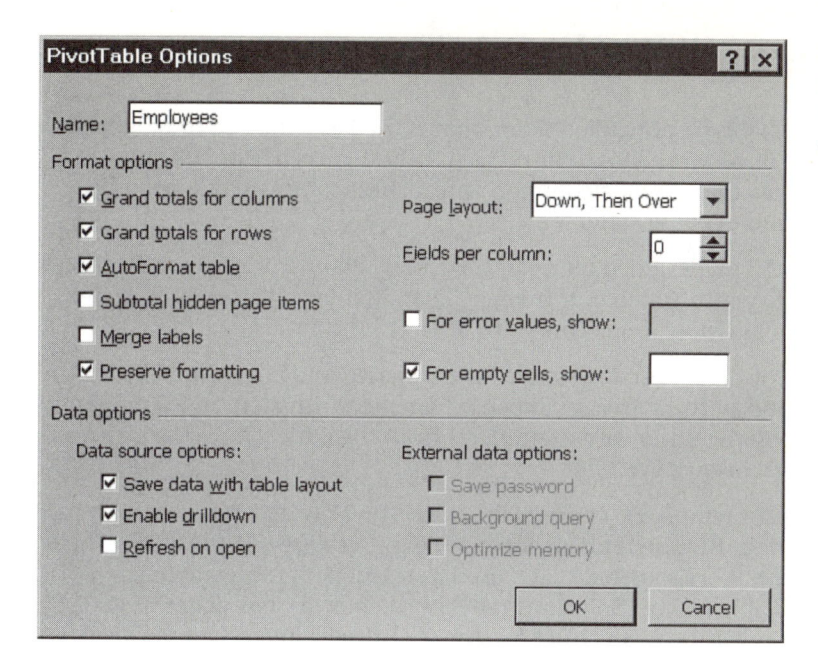

Upgrading to Microsoft Excel 95 and Excel 97

◀ **FIG. 3.24**
Excel 97 PivotTable options

FIG. 3.25 ▶
Excel 97 PivotTable toolbar

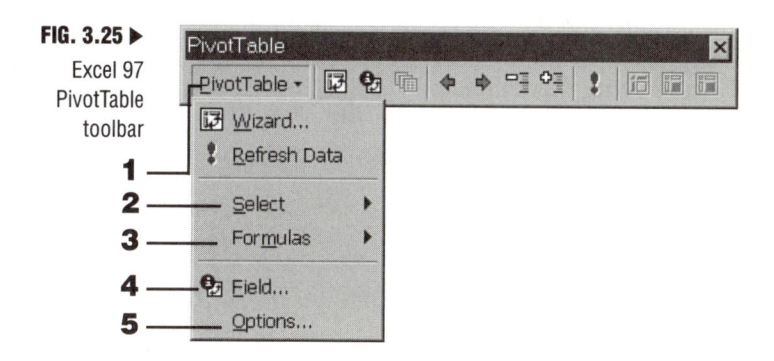

1. Wizard...
2. Select
3. Formulas
4. Field...
5. Options...

Templates
Using the Built-in Templates

A *template* is a special type of workbook file that is used as a master, or blueprint, for creating other Excel workbooks. Both Excel 95 and Excel 97 include built-in worksheet templates that provide common spreadsheet forms such as invoices, purchase orders, and expense statements.

Excel 95 contains 10 predesigned templates: Business Planner, Car Lease Advisor, Change Request, Expense Statement, Invoice, Loan Manager, Personal Budgeter, Purchase Order, Sales Quote, and Time Card.

In Excel 97, three of these templates have been updated and are included with the standard installation of the software: Expense Statement, Invoice, and Purchase Order. You can copy the other seven templates from the Office 97 CD or download them from Microsoft's Web site.

To access the built-in templates, choose File, New. The New dialog box displays a series of tabs that identify the templates available in Excel (see Figure 3.26). The **1** General tab lists the Workbook template, used as the default template for new workbooks. The **2** Spreadsheet Solutions tab lists the built-in templates. If you have upgraded from Office 95 to Office 97, the **3** Office 95 Templates tab also may be listed in the New dialog box.

In Figure 3.27, a new workbook has been created based on the built-in Invoice template. Templates can be **4** customized to fit your specific requirements. Each built-in template has an option to **5** include your company name and logo. You also can change the font and add your own comments. Most templates include **6** a toolbar to help you with the template. Some of the built-in templates include **7** a feature that enables you to add data to a database each time you complete the template form. **8** Helpful notes and tips embedded in the templates assist you in working with and customizing the templates.

Upgrading to Microsoft Excel 95 and Excel 97

FIG. 3.26 ▶
Excel 97—New dialog box

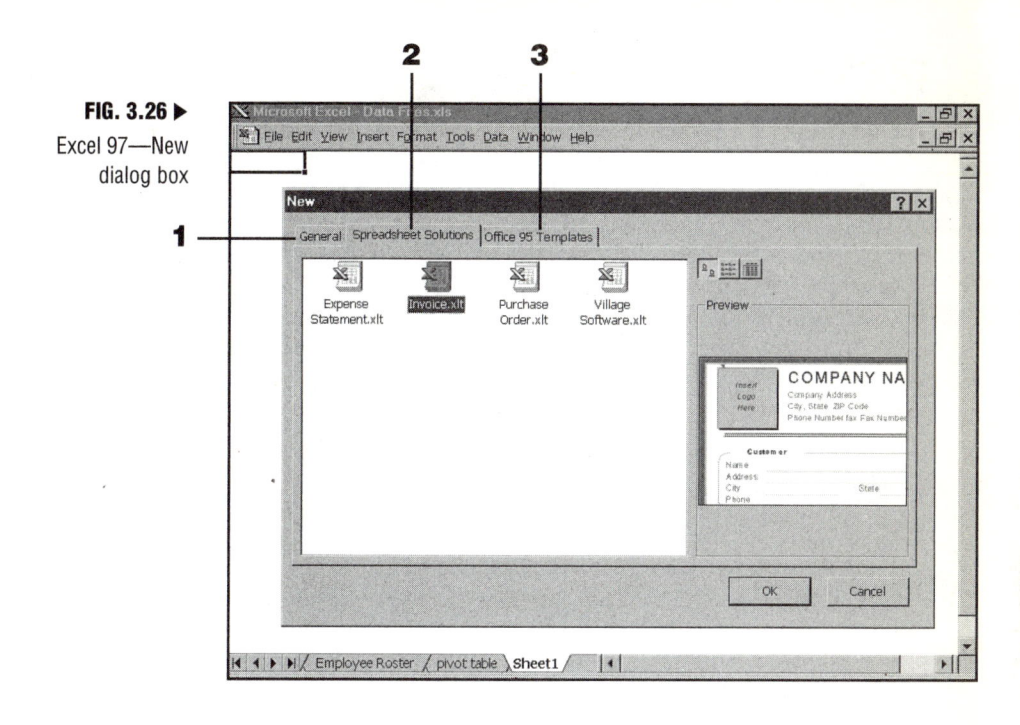

◀ FIG. 3.27
Excel 97—Invoice template

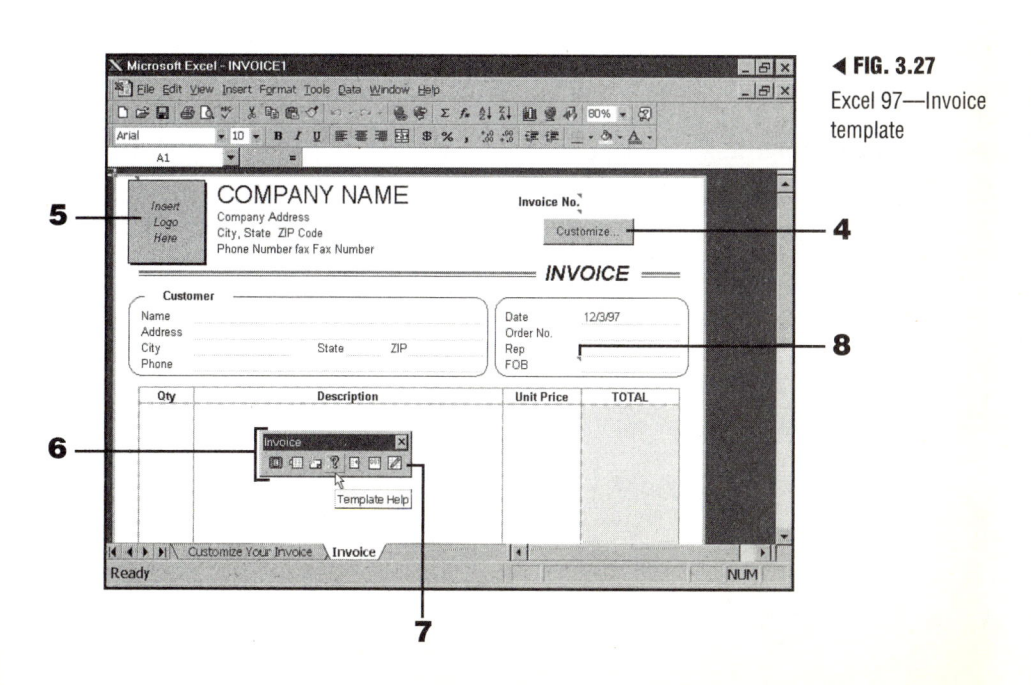

Templates

Template Wizard with Data Tracking

The Template Wizard with Data Tracking is a new add-in feature available in Excel 95 and 97. *Add-ins* are supplemental programs that add custom commands and features to Excel. The Template Wizard is used to link cells in a worksheet to fields in a database. This is particularly useful with templates that are input forms. When the form is filled in, a corresponding record is created in a database. The information in the database then can be manipulated by using the features of the database.

Some of the built-in templates include a feature that enables you to add data to a database each time you complete the template form. The data is added as a new record in a database that is associated with the template. You also can add your own custom templates that will store data into a database by using the Template Wizard with Data Tracking. The database can be a list in Excel or a database in Access, FoxPro, dBASE, or Paradox.

For example, suppose that you want to track the hours that employees worked each week on client projects. You would design a work log form on a worksheet and use the Template Wizard to create the template and links to a database. When the employee completes the work-log form, the copy of the form can be saved or printed. The completed work-log data is copied to the corresponding data fields as a new record in the database.

Additionally, you can use this feature with multiple sites that are connected by a network, where the form is linked to a central database. Store the template on a shared network drive to make it available to all users. You will need to create a shortcut to the template and make sure the shortcut is copied to the Templates folder on each user's desktop.

The Template Wizard contains five steps, with explanations to guide you through the wizard (see Figure 3.28). Follow the steps in the wizard to create the data-tracking links.

Upgrading to Microsoft Excel 95 and Excel 97

FIG. 3.28 ▶

Excel 97 Template Wizard

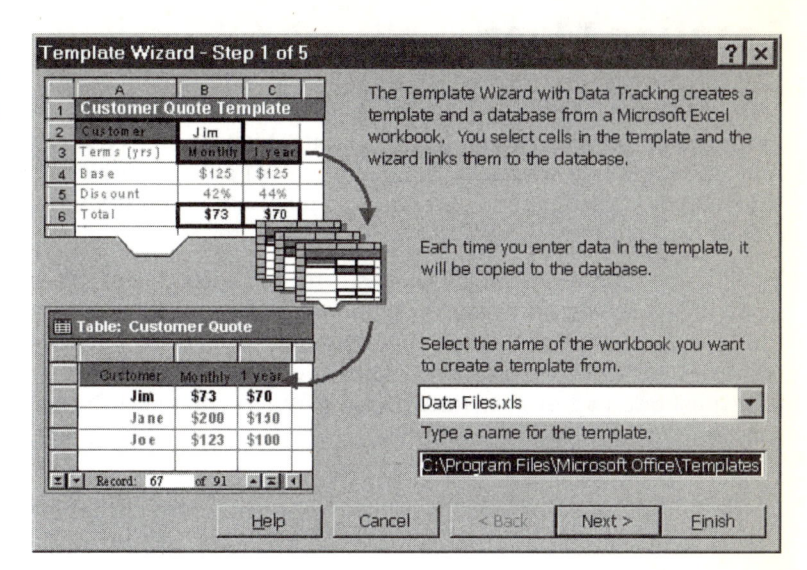

Charts and Maps
Creating Maps

New in Microsoft Excel 95 (and included in Office 97) is a feature you can use to create a map based on your worksheet data. Maps can be created to analyze sales, marketing, or any other data that is broken out geographically. The mapping feature includes demographic data, such as population and household income, that can be used along with your data.

When you create a map, the first step is to set up and select the data you want to display. Arrange the information to be mapped in columns on a worksheet. You must have at least one column that contains the names of geographic areas, countries, or states. If you want to plot additional data, such as sales figures, this data must be listed in a separate column. When you select the cells to plot in the map, include the column headings.

Figure 3.29 shows an example of a map of the United States. To use the mapping feature, select the range of cells on your worksheet and click the **1** Map button on the Standard toolbar. Then drag a rectangular shape in your worksheet where you want the map to appear.

You can change the colors and formats displayed in the map, add custom labels, or change the map's legends. For more information about working with maps, **2** click the callouts on the "Displaying data in a map" help screen (see Figure 3.30).

Upgrading to Microsoft Excel 95 and Excel 97

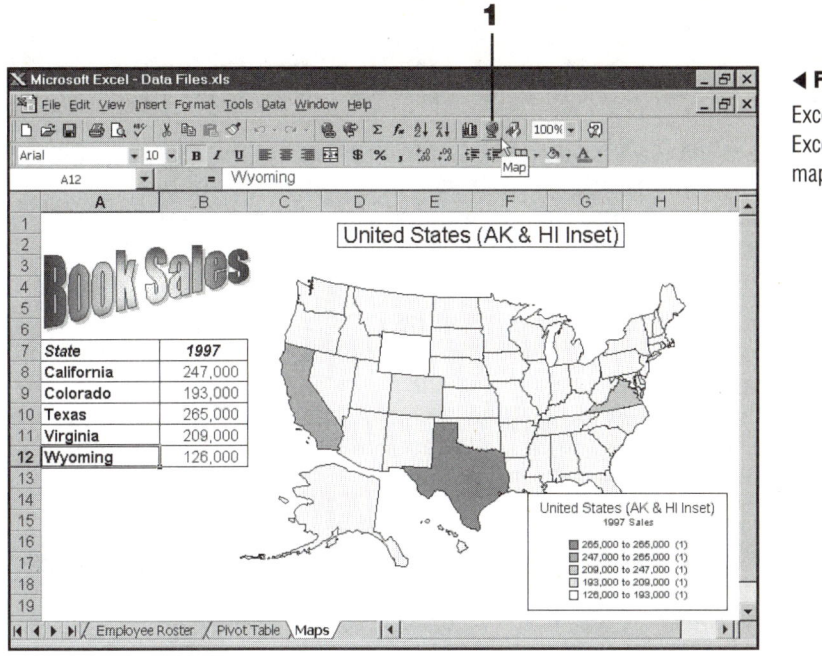

◄ **FIG. 3.29**
Excel 95 and Excel 97 sample map

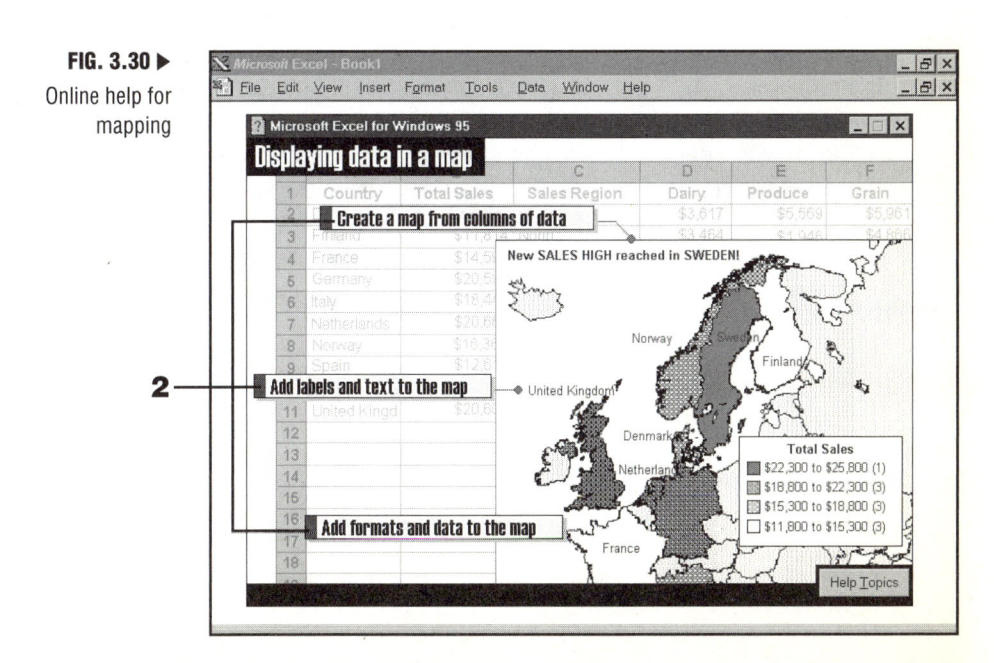

FIG. 3.30 ►
Online help for mapping

Charts and Maps
Improved Chart Wizard (Excel 97 Only)

The Chart Wizard in Excel 95 is virtually identical to and has the same capabilities as the Chart Wizard in Excel 5.0. In Excel 97, the Chart Wizard has improved greatly. You can create both embedded charts and chart sheets with the wizard. There are many new and enhanced options, and the Office Assistant is programmed to provide assistance as you build your chart.

There are 14 standard chart types available in Excel 97. The **1** Cylinder, Cone, and Pyramid chart types are variations of the column and bar charts, as shown in Figure 3.31. Figure 3.31 shows step 1 of 4 of the new Chart Wizard, with the Pyramid chart type selected. Another chart type new to Excel 97 is the Bubble, a type of scatter chart. Pie of Pie and Bar of Pie are variations of the Pie chart used to further break out specific components of a wedge of the original pie.

In addition to the standard chart types, you can use 20 custom chart types. You will find special types like Combination charts and Logarithmic charts under the custom types, as well as some of the standard chart types that have been modified with colorful backgrounds or shading.

Other improvements to charts in Excel 97 include the following:

- Easier editing of embedded charts.
- Data tables now available in charts.
- Number of data points plotted per series increased from 4,000 to 32,000.
- New formatting options, such as using pictures or texture for fills and scaling marker size. Figure 3.32 shows an example of a picture fill used in a bar chart.
- **2** Chart tips available when you rest the mouse pointer over a chart object.
- Improved display of text in charts, including **3** text rotation.

> **TIP** Excel provides a number of good chart examples through the built-in help screens: Type **chart examples** in the Office Assistant search box and choose **Examples of chart types**.

Upgrading to Microsoft Excel 95 and Excel 97

FIG. 3.31 ▶
Excel 97 Chart Wizard

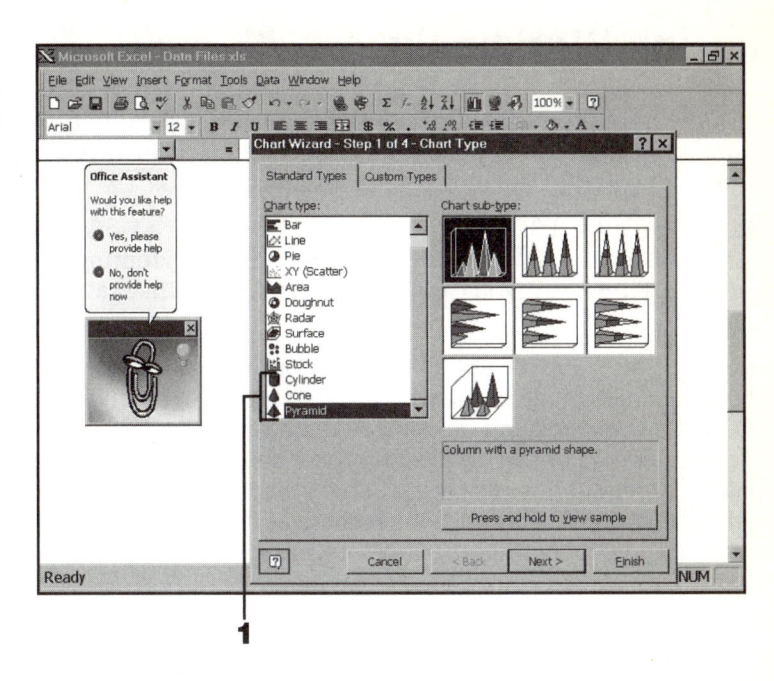

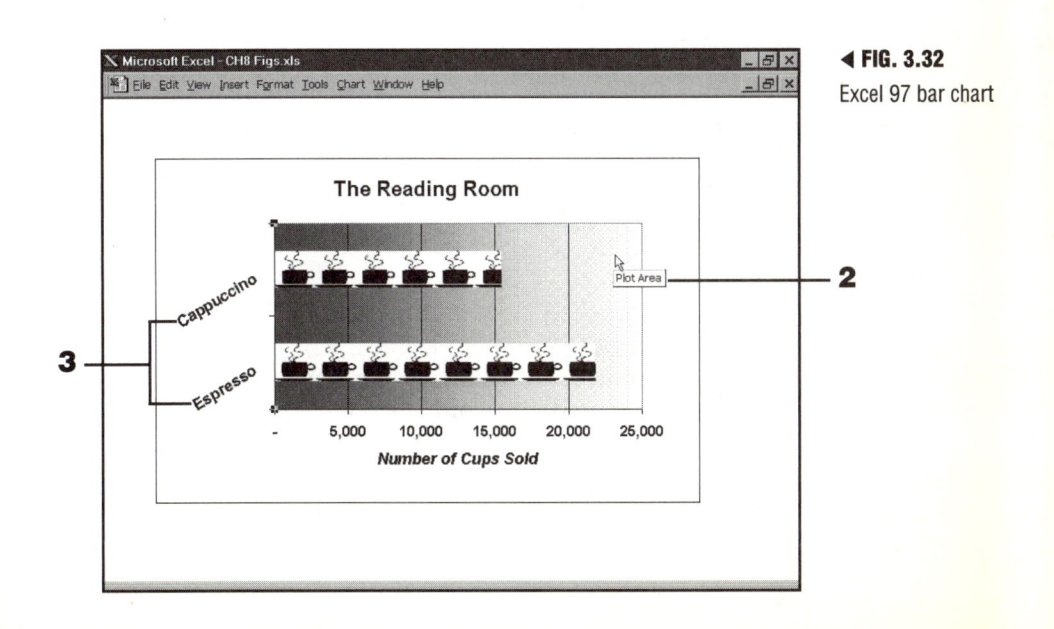

◀ FIG. 3.32
Excel 97 bar chart

93

Workgroup Features
Sharing Workbooks

One of the most productive features in Excel is the capability to share and revise workbooks with groups of people. Frequently, projects involve several people entering or verifying data in the same documents.

In Excel 5.0 (Office 4.3), your only options for sharing a workbook are saving the workbook to a network drive or electronically mailing/routing the workbook to other users. Either way, you cannot easily track what changes were made and by whom.

In Excel 95, you have the ability to share your workbooks with other users and track the changes made to the workbook. The File, Shared Lists command is used to share the workbook and determine who has the file open. With this command, you can enter data or sort data, add rows or columns, but you cannot change cell formatting or modify formulas. If changes made to the file conflict, you can see a list of conflicts and determine which changes to accept or reject. You continue to have the option of routing the workbook electronically to other users for their review.

In Excel 97, you have the ability to truly share a workbook. One person can edit one worksheet in a workbook, and someone else can edit another worksheet simultaneously. When one user saves the workbook, the other users who are sharing it will see the changes made by that user. Different people can access adjacent data in the same worksheet, such as the formulas on a worksheet and the column headings. The shared workbook feature replaces the shared list feature in Microsoft Excel 95. Excel 97 provides several options you can use when you need to coordinate workbook files with groups of people: creating a Binder file, sharing workbooks, tracking changes, and highlighting text.

> **TIP** Only Excel 97 supports the shared workbook feature. If some users in your group are still working with previous versions of Excel, they will not be able to open the shared workbook.

To share a workbook with other users in Excel 97, choose Tools, Share Workbook, and the Share Workbook dialog box appears (see Figure 3.33). The Advanced tab contains sharing options that control how changes to the shared workbook will be tracked. When a workbook is shared, the word [Shared] appears in the title bar for the workbook.

The Highlight Changes dialog box, shown in Figure 3.34, works with settings on the Advanced tab of the Share Workbook dialog box to control how changes to the shared workbook are tracked.

Upgrading to Microsoft Excel 95 and Excel 97

Each time you view the shared workbook, you need to specify how you want to review the changes in the Highlight Changes dialog box. The settings are established only for the working session; the next time you view the file, you have to specify your choices again. Some Excel commands are not available when a workbook is shared:

- **Inserting and Deleting.** Blocks of cells cannot be inserted or deleted, though you can insert or delete entire rows and columns. You can insert worksheets but cannot delete worksheets.
- **Formatting.** You cannot apply conditional formats or merged cells after a workbook has been shared.
- **List Manipulation Commands.** When you filter data in a shared workbook and make print settings you want, your settings are then saved independently of settings made by other users. Whenever you open the shared workbook, your personal settings appear. The Group and Outline, Subtotals, Tables, and PivotTable Report commands cannot be used when a workbook is shared.
- **Linked or Embedded Objects.** Charts, pictures, objects, or hyperlinks can't be modified in a shared workbook.
- **Macros.** You can only run macros that were created before you shared the workbook. New macros cannot be created.
- **Password Protection.** While a workbook is shared, you cannot create, modify, or remove passwords that protect the worksheets or the entire workbook. Any protection that is assigned to a worksheet or workbook prior to sharing the file remains in effect while the workbook is shared.
- **Scenarios.** This command can't be used while the workbook is shared.
- **Data Validation.** You can't modify or create data-validation restrictions while the workbook is shared. Any restrictions that are set up prior to sharing the workbook remain in effect.
- **Drawing.** The drawing tools can't be used after a workbook has been shared.

Most of the limitations can be implemented before sharing the workbook, and then are available after sharing the workbook.

When users make changes to your workbook, their edits are color coded. When you rest the pointer over a cell that has been modified, information is displayed about who made the change, when the change was made, and what type of change it was.

> **TIP** Excel identifies who made what changes, when in the shared workbook, based on the name of the user. To ensure accurate tracking, each user should establish his or her user name before working on the shared book. Instruct each user to choose Tools, Options and click the General tab, and then type his or her user name in the User Name box.

You can step through highlighted changes in a shared workbook and accept or reject each change. Information about how conflicts are resolved is now available on the History worksheet (the Conflicts worksheet in Excel 95). The History worksheet maintains information about any changes that are replaced by other changes. You can track the history of changes to a shared workbook for a specified amount of time. When you want to view what changes have been made to the workbook, you can display a separate filtered History worksheet.

If you reject a change, you can get it back by finding it in the History worksheet for the workbook.

> **NOTE** When you remove a workbook from shared use, the history of changes is erased. When you share the workbook again, a new list of changes is created.

Users can attach their comments directly to cells. In Excel 5.0 and Excel 95, these are called Notes. In Excel 97, they are called Comments. Figure 3.35 shows a **1** shared workbook with several **2** embedded comments. One of the features added to Comments in Excel 97 is the **3** Reviewing toolbar. You can use this toolbar to make sure you've read all the comments by stepping through the comments in a workbook in sequence.

FIG. 3.33 ▶
Excel 97—Share Workbook dialog box

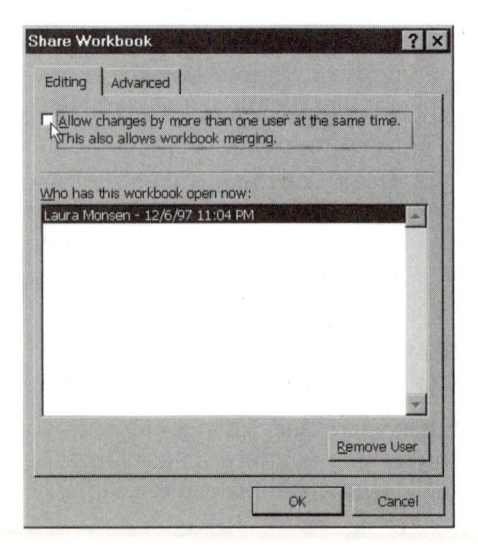

Upgrading to Microsoft Excel 95 and Excel 97

FIG. 3.34 ▶
Excel 97—
Highlight Changes
dialog box

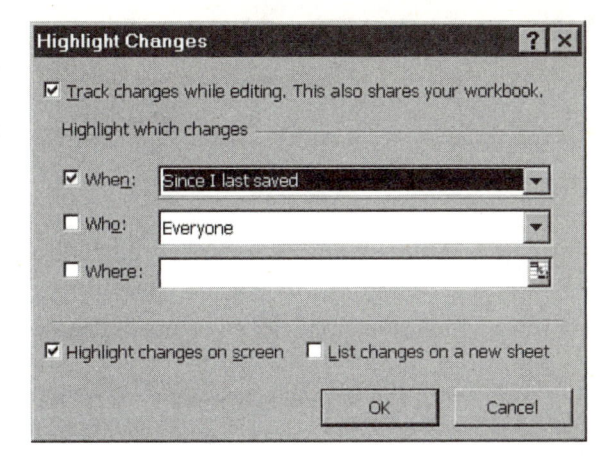

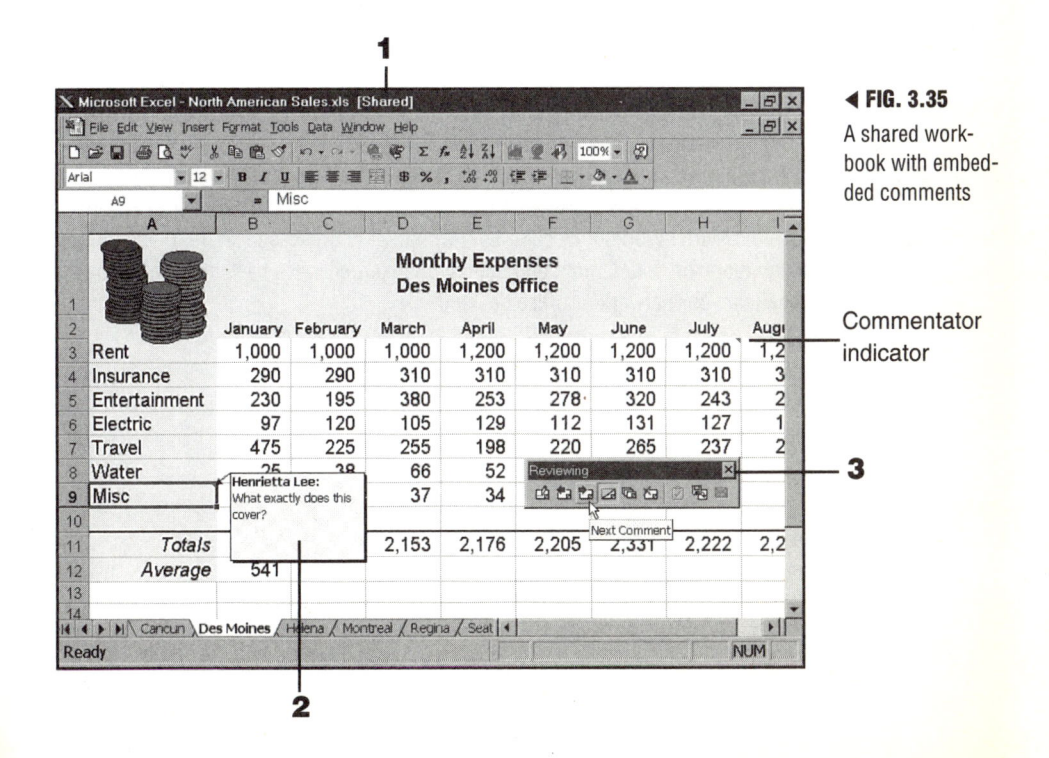

◀ FIG. 3.35
A shared workbook with embedded comments

Commentator indicator

97

Workgroup Features
Merging Workbooks (Excel 97 Only)

Instead of sharing a workbook with other users, you can provide separate copies of a workbook to users and then merge the copies, along with any comments or changes, into one workbook file. This feature is not available to Excel 5.0 and Excel 95 users.

Before you distribute copies of the workbook for review and editing, there are several things to consider:

- The workbook from which the copies are to be made must be a shared workbook.
- All copies must come from the same workbook but must have unique filenames.
- Before the copies are made, the change history in the original workbook must be turned on (choose the Advanced tab in the Share Workbooks dialog box). Then the merge must be completed within the time period you specified to maintain the history. If you aren't sure how long the review process will take, make sure you enter a large number of days, such as 500.
- The workbooks either must not have passwords or must both have the same password.

When workbooks are merged, comments on a cell from different users are identified by individual user names and are merged into a single comment box. Choose Tools, Merge Workbooks to merge your workbooks (see Figure 3.36).

> **NOTE** You can use the Merge Workbooks command with the My Briefcase feature to edit a copy of a workbook on your laptop, and then merge your changes back into the copy of the workbook on your network or office desktop.

FIG. 3.36 ▶

Excel 97—Select Files to Merge Into Current Workbook dialog box

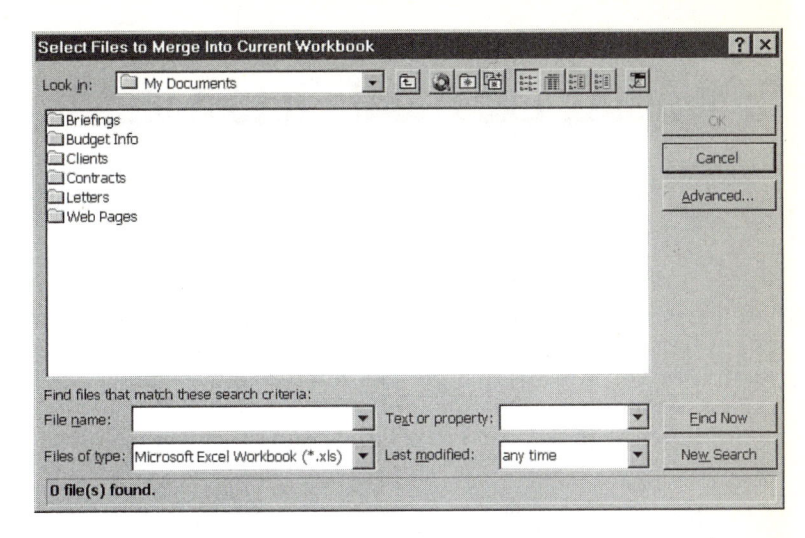

Importing and Exporting Data
Converting Excel Data into Access

You can import files from many different programs by simply using the File, Open command. Excel files can be exported to other programs by saving them in other file formats through the File, Save As command. This feature is available in all versions of Excel.

Both Excel 95 and Excel 97 come with the capability to create Access forms and reports based on your Excel worksheets, while you are in Excel. The AccessLinks Add-In contains wizards that prompt you through the process of creating Access forms and reports. Additionally, this add-in includes the Convert to Access command, which enables you to move data from Excel worksheets to an Access database.

In Excel 95, the AccessLinks Add-In is automatically installed and is comprised of three commands on the Data menu: Access Form, Access Report, and Convert to Access.

In Excel 97, you will have to install the AccessLinks Add-In. Choose Tools, Add-Ins and select AccessLinks from the Add-In dialog box. The MS Access Form, MS Access Report, and Convert to MS Access commands will then be added to the Data menu.

The Access Form and Access Report commands work similarly. When you select one of these commands, it launches a wizard. The wizard will guide you through building a data entry form or a report based on your Excel list. To create the form or report, a table will be created in Access based on the data in your Excel list. When you select either the Access Form or Access Report command, a dialog box appears asking whether you want to create the form or report in a new Access database or an existing Access database. Figure 3.37 shows the Create Microsoft Access Form dialog box. The Create Microsoft Access Report dialog box is identical, except for the title of the dialog box.

> **NOTE** Your data must be organized as a list (or database) in Excel before you attempt to use the Access Form or Access Report commands. An Excel list begins with a row of headings and cannot contain any empty rows or columns. The headings will be used by Access as field names in the new table.

Once you have made your selections in the dialog box, the **1** Access program is opened, and a table based on your Excel list is created. Then the Form or Report Wizard starts, using the **2** newly created table. Figure 3.38 shows the first step in the Access Form Wizard. Figure 3.39 shows the first step in the Access Report Wizard.

After the form or report is created, the wizard adds a button to your Excel worksheet. You can modify the form or report by using this button.

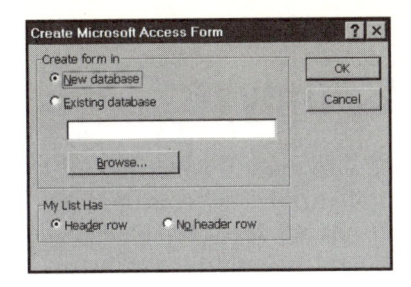

Upgrading to Microsoft Excel 95 and Excel 97

◄ FIG. 3.37
Excel 97—Access Form Wizard

FIG. 3.38 ►
Excel 97—Select the fields to include in the form

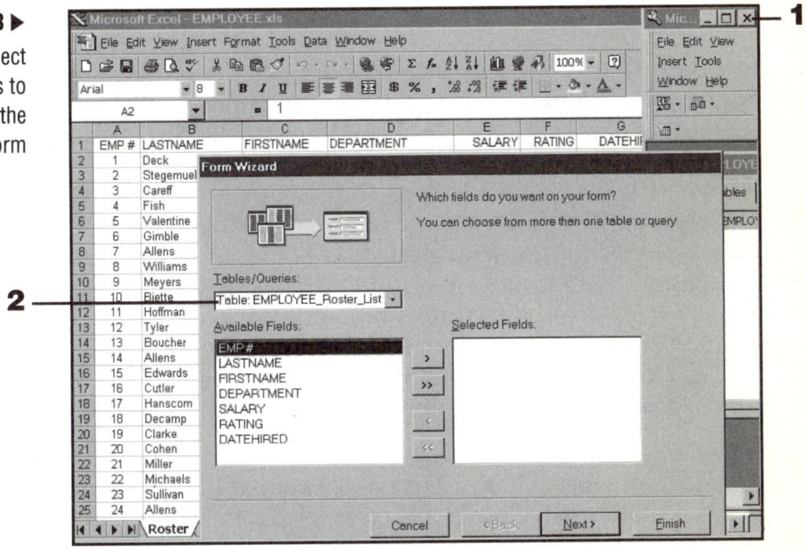

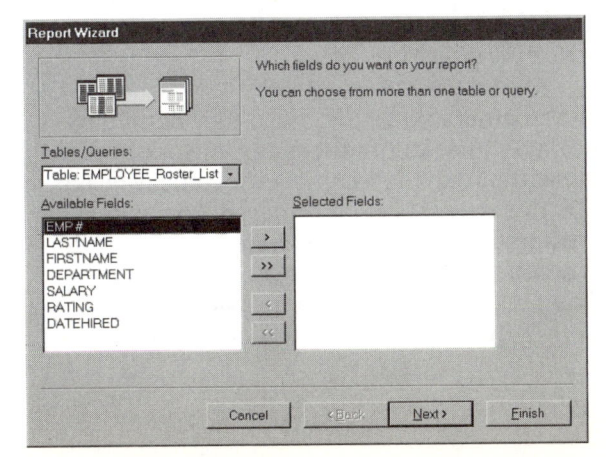

◄ FIG. 3.39
Excel 97—Select the fields to include in the report

101

Importing and Exporting Data
Enhanced MS Query (Excel 97 Only)

An extremely powerful feature of Excel is the capability to retrieve data from external sources so that it can be analyzed and manipulated by the tools in Excel. Microsoft Query has been available in Excel since version 5.0. It is a separate program that comes with Microsoft Office and that works with Excel to make it easy to retrieve data from databases and copy the data into an Excel worksheet. You can then use any of the tools Excel provides, such as pivot tables and charting, to work with the list of data. In Excel 97, the integration between Microsoft Query and Excel has been improved.

You can access Microsoft Query directly from Excel to retrieve specific information from external sources, primarily databases. Some examples of the programs you can retrieve data from include Access, FoxPro, dBASE, Paradox, and SQL Server. In Excel 97, you also can retrieve information from the Internet by using HTML filters. The data can be filtered, sorted, formatted, or edited in Microsoft Query *before* it is inserted into your worksheet. The data can be retrieved by using either the Query Wizard, a new interface in Microsoft Query available only in Excel 97, or directly from the Microsoft Query window using Excel 95 or Excel 97. The Query Wizard helps you create quick and simple query designs to retrieve data; use it when you want to retrieve data from only *one table* in a database. If you want to retrieve data from *multiple tables* in a database, the Microsoft Query window enables you to work in more detail to customize and view your data retrieval.

To start Microsoft Query, choose Data, Get External Data, Create New Query. The Choose Data Source dialog box appears, as shown in Figure 3.40.

> **NOTE** Microsoft Query is an optional feature in Microsoft Excel and may not be installed on your computer. If a warning message appears when you select Create New Query, then Microsoft Query is not installed. You will have to install Microsoft Query from the Microsoft Office disks or CD before you can proceed.

You can create and distribute queries to other Excel 97 users, so they don't have to repeat the steps of setting up the data source to run the query. A worksheet can be saved with a query as a template, without saving a copy of the retrieved data. When you open the report template, the external data is retrieved. You will be prompted for a password if one is required. Queries can be created that prompt you for parameters each time they're run, so that you can create more flexible queries and work with larger databases. Queries now run in the background so that you can continue to work on other things in Excel while data is being retrieved.

FIG. 3.40 ▶
Excel 97—
Choose Data
Source dialog box

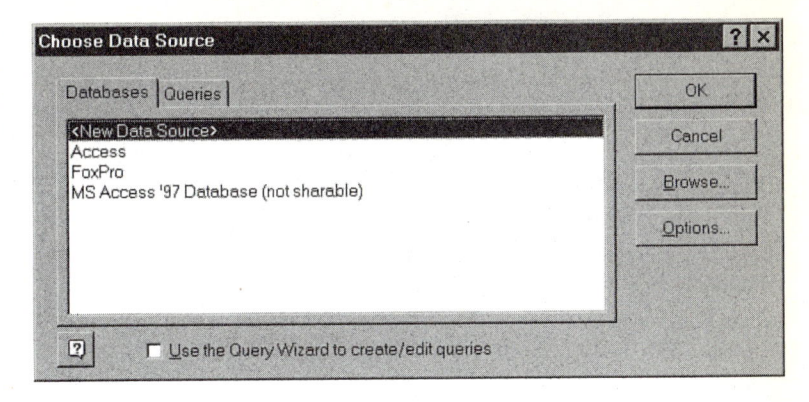

Index

A

Accept or Reject Changes dialog box (Word), 52
Access, converting Excel data to, 100-101
Access Links add-in (Excel), 100-101
add-ins (Excel), 88, 100-101
Advanced Find dialog box, 4-5
Advanced Search dialog box, 4-5
animation of fonts (Word 97), 44-45
annotations, inserting (Word 95), 48
Answer Wizard, 14
AutoComplete feature
   Excel, 70-71
   Word, 20
AutoCorrect dialog box, 8-9
AutoFilter feature (Excel), 82-83
AutoFormat feature (Word), 20
AutoSummarize feature (Word), 21
AVERAGEA function (Excel 97), 80-81

B

borders for tables (Word), 30-31
Borders toolbar (Word 95), 30-31
built-in templates, creating files
   Excel, 62-63, 86-87
   Word, 24-25, 38-39

C

cells (Excel 97)
   comments, inserting, 76-77, 96
   conditional formatting, 74-75
   data
      indenting, 68-69
      rotating, 68-69
      validating, 72-73
   merging, 66-67
Cells command (Format menu), Excel, 68-69
Change Text Direction button, Tables and Borders toolbar (Word 97), 36-37
Chart Wizard, new features (Excel 97), 92-93
Choose Data Source dialog box (Excel), 102-103
columns in tables, distributing evenly in Word 97, 34-35
commands
   Data menu (Excel)
      Get External Data, 102
      Validation, 72-73

File menu (Excel)
   New, 62, 86-87
   Page Setup, 76
   Save As HTML, 64-65
   Shared Lists, 94
File menu (Word)
   New, 24-25, 38-39
   Save As, 40-41
   Save As HTML, 26-27
   Versions, 54-55
Format menu (Excel)
   Cells, 68-69
   Conditional Formatting, 74-75
Format menu (Word), Font, 42-45
Insert menu (Excel)
   Comment, 76
   Note, 76
Insert menu (Word), Comment, 48
Table menu (Word), Draw Table, 32-33
Tools menu (Excel)
   Merge Workbooks, 98
   Share Workbook, 94
Tools menu (Word)
   Merge Documents, 50-51
   Options, 46-47
   Revisions, 46-47
   Track Changes, 46-47
View menu (Word), Comments, 48
Comment command (Insert menu)
   Excel, 76
   Word, 48

Index

comments
  inserting
    Excel, 76-77, 96
    Word 97, 48
  printing (Excel), 76

Comments command (View menu), Word, 48

conditional formatting of cells (Excel 97), 74-75

Conditional Formatting command (Format menu), Excel, 74-75

Conditional Formatting dialog box, Excel, 74-75

Contents tab (Help Topics dialog box), 12-13

converting
  Excel data to Access, 100-101
  files between versions
    Excel, 60-61
    Word, 22-23

custom templates, creating in Word, 40-41

D

data
  converting to Access from Excel, 100-101
  indenting (Excel 97), 68-69
  maps, creating (Excel), 90-91
  rotating (Excel 97), 68-69
  validating (Excel 97), 72-73

Data menu commands (Excel)
  Get External Data, 102
  Validation, 72-73

Data Validation dialog box (Excel), 72-73

databases
  importing Excel data to, 100-101
  linking worksheets with, 88-89
  queries to (Microsoft Query), 102-103

dialog boxes
  Accept or Reject Changes (Word), 52
  Advanced Find, 4-5
  Advanced Search, 4-5
  AutoCorrect, 8-9
  Choose Data Source (Excel), 102-103
  Conditional Formatting (Excel), 74-75
  Data Validation (Excel), 72-73
  Find All Files, 4-5
  Font (Word), 42-45
  Format Cells (Excel), 66-69
  Help Topics, new features, 12-13
  Highlight Changes
    Excel, 94, 97
    Word, 46-47
  New
    Excel, 62, 86-87
    Word, 24-25, 38-41
  Open, new features, 2-3
  Options (Word), 46-47
  Page Setup (Excel), 76
  Paste Function (Excel), 78-79
  PivotTable Options (Excel), 84
  Review Revisions (Word), 52

  Revisions (Word), 47
  Save As
    new features, 6
    Word, 40-41
  Save As HTML (Word), 26-27
  Save Version (Word), 54-55
  Select File to Merge Into Current Document (Word), 50-51
  Select Files to Merge Into Current Workbook (Excel), 99
  Share Workbook (Excel), 94, 96
  Spelling and Grammar (Word), 28-29
  Versions In (Word), 54-55

Distribute Columns Evenly feature (Word 97), 34-35

Distribute Rows Evenly feature (Word 97), 34-35

documents
  comments, inserting (Word 97), 48
  merging (Word 97), 50-51
  revisions, reviewing changes (Word), 52-53
  saving versions of (Word 97), 54-55
  versions (Word), 21
  see also files

downloading Word 97 file converter, 22

Draw Table command (Table menu), Word, 32-33

105

drawing tables in
  Word 97, 32-33
Drawing toolbar
  (Office Art), 10-11

E

editing formulas
  (Excel 97), 78-79
Excel, 57
  AutoComplete feature,
    70-71
  comments
    inserting, 76-77, 96
    printing, 76
  creating files with
    templates, 62-63,
    86-87
  data, converting to
    Access, 100-101
  exchanging files
    between versions,
    60-61
  History worksheet, 96
  lists, filtering, 82-83
  maps, creating, 90-91
  pivot tables, 84
  templates (Template
    Wizard with Data
    Tracking), 88-89
  workbooks, sharing,
    94-95, 97
Excel 95, new
  features, 58
Excel 97
  cells
    *conditional
      formatting, 74-75*
    merging, 66-67
  Chart Wizard, new
    features, 92-93
  data
    indenting, 68-69
    rotating, 68-69
    validating, 72-73

formulas, creating/
  editing, 78-79
Microsoft Query, new
  features, 102-103
new features, 58-59
new functions in,
  80-81
saving files in HTML
  format, 64-65
workbooks, merging,
  98-99
exchanging files
  between versions
  Excel, 60-61
  Word, 22-23
exporting/
  importing data
  between Excel and
    Access, 100-101
  to Excel with Microsoft
    Query, 102-103

F

File menu commands
  New
    Excel, 62, 86-87
    Word, 24-25, 38-39
  Page Setup (Excel), 76
  Save As (Word), 40-41
  Save As HTML
    Excel, 64-65
    Word, 26-27
  Shared Lists (Excel), 94
  Versions (Word), 54-55
files
  converting to Access
    from Excel, 100-101
  creating with templates
    Excel, 62-63, 86-87
    Word, 24-25, 38-39
  exchanging between
    versions
    Excel, 60-61
    Word, 22-23

finding, 4-5
opening, 2-3
previewing, 2
saving, 6
  *in HTML format,
    26-27, 64-65*
  versions of, 21
  see also documents
filtering lists (Excel),
  82-83
Find All Files dialog box,
  4-5
Find tab (Help Topics
  dialog box), 12-13
finding files, 4-5
Font command (Format
  menu), Word, 42-45
Font dialog box (Word),
  42-45
fonts
  advanced effects
    (Word 97), 42-43
  animation (Word 97),
    44-45
Format Cells dialog box
  (Excel), 66-69
Format menu
  commands
  Cells (Excel), 68-69
  Conditional Formatting
    (Excel), 74-75
  Font (Word), 42-45
formatting
  cells, conditional
    formatting (Excel 97),
    74-75
  tables (Word), 21
  text (Word), 21
formulas
  creating/editing
    (Excel 97), 78-79
  new functions
    (Excel 97), 80-81

106

Index

functions
 new in Excel 97, 80-81
 Paste Function dialog box (Excel), 78-79

G-H

Get External Data command (Data menu), Excel, 102

GETPIVOTDATA function (Excel 97), 80

grammar checking in Word, 28-29

help
 Answer Wizard, 14
 Office Assistant, 14
 table of contents, new features, 12-13
 via the Web, 16-17

Help Topics dialog box, new features, 12-13

Highlight Changes dialog box
 Excel, 94, 97
 Word, 46-47

highlighting text (Word), 20

History worksheet (Excel), 96

HTML format, saving files
 Excel 97, 64-65
 Word 97, 26-27

HYPERLINK function (Excel 97), 80

I-J

images for Office Assistant, changing, 14

importing/ exporting data
 between Excel and Access, 100-101
 to Excel with Microsoft Query, 102-103

indenting data (Excel 97), 68-69

Index tab (Help Topics dialog box), 12-13

Insert menu commands
 Comment
  Excel, 76
  Word, 48
 Note (Excel), 76

inserting comments
 Excel, 76-77, 96
 Word 97, 48

Internet
 features in Word, 21
 online help via, 16-17

Internet Assistant Wizard, saving files as HTML, 64-65

K-L

linking worksheets with databases, 88-89

lists, filtering (Excel), 82-83

locating files, 4-5

M

macros, warning about, 62

maps, creating (Excel), 90-91

MAXA function (Excel 97), 80

Merge Documents command (Tools menu), Word, 50-51

Merge Workbooks command (Tools menu), Excel, 98

merging
 cells (Excel 97), 66-67
 documents (Word 97), 50-51
 workbooks (Excel 97), 98-99

Microsoft Excel, 57
 AutoComplete feature, 70-71
 comments
  inserting, 76-77, 96
  printing, 76
 creating files with templates, 62-63, 86-87
 data, converting to Access, 100-101
 exchanging files between versions, 60-61
 History worksheet, 96
 lists, filtering, 82-83
 maps, creating, 90-91
 pivot tables, 84
 templates (Template Wizard with Data Tracking), 88-89
 workbooks, sharing, 94-95, 97
 see also Excel 95; Excel 97

Microsoft Office, new features, 1
 Answer Wizard, 14
 AutoCorrect, 8-9
 finding files, 4-5
 Office Art, 10-11
 Office Assistant, 14

107

online help, 12-13
opening files, 2-3
saving files, 6
Web online help, 16-17

Microsoft Query, new features, 102-103

Microsoft Word, 19
  AutoComplete feature, 20
  AutoFormat feature, 20
  AutoSummarize feature, 21
  borders on tables, 30-31
  creating files with templates, 24-25, 38-39
  document versions, 21
  exchanging files between versions, 22-23
  formatting
    tables, 21
    text, 21
  highlighting text, 20
  Internet features, 21
  revisions, reviewing changes, 52-53
  spell-checking, 20, 28-29
  templates, 20
    creating custom, 40-41
  Tip Wizard, 20
  virus alert, 21
  Visual Basic, 21
  see also Word 95; Word 97

MINA function (Excel 97), 80

N

New command (File menu)
  Excel, 62, 86-87
  Word, 24-25, 38-39

New dialog box
  Excel, 62, 86-87
  Word, 24-25, 38-41

Note command (Insert menu), Excel, 76

notes, inserting (Excel), 76-77, 96

O

Office, *see* Microsoft Office

Office Art, 10-11

Office Assistant, 14
  images, changing, 14

online help
  Answer Wizard, 14
  Office Assistant, 14
  table of contents, new features, 12-13
  via the Web, 16-17

Open dialog box, new features, 2-3

opening files, 2-3

Options command (Tools menu), Word, 46-47

Options dialog box (Word), 46-47

orientation of text, changing in tables (Word 97), 36-37

P

Page Setup command (File menu), Excel, 76

Page Setup dialog box (Excel), 76

Paste Function dialog box (Excel), 78-79

pivot tables (Excel), 84

PivotTable Options dialog box (Excel), 84

PivotTable toolbar (Excel), 84

previewing files, 2

printing comments (Excel), 76

Q-R

queries to databases (Microsoft Query), 102-103

Query Wizard (Excel), 102

Review Revisions dialog box (Word), 52

reviewing document changes (Word), 52-53

Reviewing toolbar (Word), 48

revisions
  merging documents (Word 97), 50-51
  reviewing changes (Word), 52-53
  tracking changes (Word 97), 46-47

Index

Revisions command (Tools menu), Word, 46-47

Revisions dialog box (Word), 47

rotating data (Excel 97), 68-69

rows in tables, distributing evenly in Word 97, 34-35

S

Save As command (File menu), Word, 40-41

Save As dialog box
new features, 6
Word, 40-41

Save As HTML command (File menu)
Excel, 64-65
Word, 26-27

Save As HTML dialog box (Word), 26-27

Save Version dialog box (Word), 54-55

saving
document versions (Word 97), 54-55
files, 6
in HTML format, 26-27, 64-65
versions of, 21

searching for files, 4-5

Select File to Merge Into Current Document dialog box (Word), 50-51

Select Files to Merge Into Current Workbook dialog box (Excel), 99

Share Workbook command (Tools menu), Excel, 94

Share Workbook dialog box (Excel), 94, 96

Shared Lists command (File menu), Excel, 94

sharing workbooks (Excel), 94-95, 97

spell-checking in Word, 20, 28-29

Spelling and Grammar dialog box (Word), 28-29

Split Cells button, Table and Borders toolbar (Word), 32

STDEVA function (Excel 97), 80

STDEVPA function (Excel 97), 80

T

Table and Borders toolbar (Word 97), 30-31

Table menu commands (Word), Draw Table, 32-33

table of contents (online help), new features, 12-13

tables
borders (Word), 30-31
changing text orientation (Word 97), 36-37
distributing columns/rows evenly (Word 97), 34-35
drawing (Word 97), 32-33
formatting (Word), 21

Template Wizard with Data Tracking (Excel), 88-89

templates
creating custom (Word), 40-41
creating files
Excel, 62-63, 86-87
Word, 24-25, 38-39
macros, warning about, 62
Template Wizard with Data Tracking (Excel), 88-89
Word, 20

text
AutoComplete feature (Excel), 70-71
comments, inserting (Word 97), 48
font animation (Word 97), 44-45
font effects (Word 97), 42-43
formatting (Word), 21
highlighting (Word), 20
revisions
merging documents (Word 97), 50-51
reviewing changes (Word 97), 52-53
tracking changes (Word 97), 46-47
spell-checking (Word), 28-29
in tables, changing orientation (Word 97), 36-37

Tip Wizard (Word), 20

toolbars
Borders (Word 95), 30-31

109

Drawing (Office Art), 10-11
PivotTable (Excel), 84
Reviewing (Word), 48
Table and Borders (Word 97), 30-31

Tools menu commands
Merge Documents (Word), 50-51
Merge Workbooks (Excel), 98
Options (Word), 46-47
Revisions (Word), 46-47
Share Workbook (Excel), 94
Track Changes (Word), 46-47

Track Changes command (Tools menu), Word, 46-47

U-V

User Information tab, Options dialog box (Word), 46-47

validating data (Excel 97), 72-73

Validation command (Data menu), Excel, 72-73

VARA function (Excel 97), 80

VARPA function (Excel 97), 80

versions
documents (Word), 21
saving (Word 97), 54-55
Excel, exchanging files between, 60-61

Word, exchanging files between, 22-23

Versions command (File menu), Word, 54-55

Versions In dialog box (Word), 54-55

View menu commands (Word), Comments, 48

virus alert (Word), 21

Visual Basic, 21

W-Z

warning about macros, 62

Web, online help via, 16-17

wizards
AccessLinks add-in (Excel), 100-101
Answer Wizard, 14
Chart Wizard, new features (Excel 97), 92-93
Internet Assistant Wizard, saving files as HTML, 64-65
Query Wizard (Excel), 102
Template Wizard with Data Tracking (Excel), 88-89
templates (Word), 38-39
Tip Wizard (Word), 20

Word, 19
AutoComplete feature, 20
AutoFormat feature, 20
AutoSummarize feature, 21
borders on tables, 30-31

creating files with templates, 24-25, 38-39
document versions, 21
exchanging files between versions, 22-23
formatting
  tables, 21
  text, 21
highlighting text, 20
Internet features, 21
revisions, reviewing changes, 52-53
spell-checking, 20, 28-29
templates, 20
  creating custom, 40-41
Tip Wizard, 20
virus alert, 21
Visual Basic, 21

Word 95, new features, 20

Word 97
comments, inserting, 48
documents
  merging, 50-51
  saving versions of, 54-55
font animation, 44-45
font effects, 42-43
new features, 20-21
revisions, tracking changes, 46-47
saving files in HTML format, 26-27
tables
  changing text orientation, 36-37
  distributing columns/rows evenly, 34-35
  drawing, 32-33

Index

Word 97 file converter, downloading, 22

workbooks
- merging (Excel 97), 98-99
- sharing (Excel), 94-95, 97

worksheets
- AutoComplete feature, 70-71
- cells (Excel 97)
  - *conditional formatting,* 74-75
  - *merging,* 66-67
- Chart Wizard (Excel 97), new features, 92-93

comments
- *inserting,* 76-77, 96
- *printing,* 76

creating files with templates, 62-63, 86-87

data (Excel 97)
- *converting to Access,* 100-101
- *indenting,* 68-69
- *rotating,* 68-69
- *validating,* 72-73

exchanging files between versions, 60-61

formulas (Excel 97), creating/editing, 78-79

History, 96

linking with databases, 88-89

lists, filtering, 82-83

maps, creating, 90-91

Microsoft Query, new features, 102-103

pivot tables, 84

saving files in HTML format (Excel 97), 64-65

templates (Template Wizard with Data Tracking), 88-89

111